THE LIMITS AND DIVISIONS
OF EUROPEAN HISTORY

THE LIMITS AND DIVISIONS OF EUROPEAN HISTORY

by

OSCAR HALECKI

UNIVERSITY OF NOTRE DAME PRESS · 1962

TO MY WIFE

Preface

IT SEEMS paradoxical to say that European history has always been a neglected subject, but if we accept Professor Halecki's definition of European history as " the history of all European nations considered as a whole, as a community clearly distinct from any other ", we shall find that of the vast number of books nominally concerned with European history very few indeed satisfy the definition. We have books by the hundred thousand dealing with the history of the nationalities and states which belong to the European community; we have books dealing with world history from a European standpoint; but the histories of Europe itself as a distinct and autonomous community are so few that they can be counted on one's fingers.

It is easy to understand this state of things in the past when Europe was regarded as the civilized world, so that the history of Europe became merged in a universal history of human progress as we see in the case of Gibbon or Condorcet. But this attitude was already out of date in the nineteenth century, and the immense advance of historical studies in that age provided no lack of material for a comprehensive study of Europe as a whole. Unfortunately the growth of political nationalism and the romantic cult of nationalist ideologies proved as fatal to the study of European history as they were to the hope of a European order. Every people was so intent on asserting the uniqueness of its historical achievement and the self-sufficiency of its cultural tradition that they had no time to understand the nature of Europe herself or to appreciate the common European achievement.

Today the situation has entirely changed. The idea of European unity is no longer regarded as a vague utopian ideal: it has become a living political issue which is likely to be the centre of international discussion in the immediate future. For now that Europe has ceased to be the mistress of the world the nations of Europe have suddenly realized their need of one another and of some common bond to protect them from social disintegration and economic collapse before the pressure of rival world empires, each of which is larger than the whole of Europe put together.

The pessimists may say that it is already too late—that we can never recapture the opportunities that were lost during the nineteenth century and again for the second time in the period between the wars. But whatever the political future of Europe may be, the need for historical understanding remains. For even if Europe should undergo a process of disintegration like that of the Hellenistic world, the tradition of European culture will still survive and will continue to influence the civilization of the modern world in somewhat the same way that Hellenism continued to influence the civilization of the ancient world in the age of the Roman Empire.

It is this clear recognition of the mission of Europe in the new post-European age which distinguishes the work of Professor Halecki from that of other writers on the subject: from the pessimism of the good Europeans who regard the passing of Europe as the downfall of the whole tradition of Western civilization, and from the facile optimism of those who put their faith in the coming of a new global civilization based on the common way of life of the Common Man. His book is the only one that is known to me—perhaps the only one in existence—which answers the question—What is Europe?—in a way that does justice to the complexity of the problem without losing sight of any of the relevant factors. This is partly due to the fact that he approaches the subject from a different point of view from other historians: and with a special knowledge of those aspects of European history that have been forgotten or underestimated by Western historians—above all the development of the peoples and states of Eastern Europe in the formative period of the European state system from the fourteenth to the sixteenth century.

The neglect of this field of study by Western historians is apt to have a serious effect on our understanding of the whole European problem, since it has led to a false or oversimplified conception of the division between East and West which is reflected in current misconceptions of contemporary international problems. Thus the nationalist ideologies of the nineteenth century gave birth to a series of simplifications of history—Pan-Germanism, Pan-Slavism, even Pan-Turanianism—and though these were mutually inconsistent and contradictory, their cumulative effect was to accentuate and to exaggerate the cleavage between Eastern and Western Europe until it became fatal to the existence of the European community.

In reality the division between East and West has never followed racial frontiers. As Professor Halecki shows, Eastern Europe in the Middle Ages was a society of peoples and kingdoms, similar in political structure to the multi-national society of Western Europe and sharing a common cultural and religious tradition with it. It was only in proportion as this older Eastern Europe was conquered and absorbed by the great military empires—a process which only reached its climax in the nineteenth century—that its rich and complex international relations were superseded by the sharp dualism of conflicting power groups. In this new situation Slavophils and Pan-Germans became the propagandists of rival imperialisms and the genuine claims of the suppressed nationalities were used by either party to inflame the conflict. Yet it must be obvious to anyone who views the history of Eastern Europe as a whole that the conflict is an artificial one based on a whole series of misconceptions and simplifications. The culture of Eastern Europe was never the exclusive creation of a single people or even a single race. It was the result of a complex process of development in which influences from the Mediterranean and the Baltic crossed and mingled with those from Western Europe and from the East. Even the clash of rival empires which resulted from the westward expansion of Russia and the eastward expansion of Prussia in the eighteenth century did not represent any profound cultural divergence between East and West, but was the result of the parallel development of new types of imperialism which had more in common with one another than with the older Eastern European states which they replaced.

It is Professor Halecki's thesis that Eastern Europe is no less European than Western Europe—that both alike are integral parts of one great community of peoples, sharing the same spiritual ideals and the same cultural traditions. It is true that owing to its geographical position Eastern Europe has been more exposed than the West to external dangers, so that its development has been interrupted by catastrophic changes, like the Mongol conquest of the thirteenth century and the Turkish conquest in the later middle ages, which caused parts of Eastern Europe to be separated for centuries from the rest of the European community. So too today, it is Eastern Europe which has had to bear the brunt of the totalitarian attack. But this is a danger that menaces Western Europe also, and as there are forces in Western Europe that favour the totalitarian revolution, so also in Eastern Europe the forces of freedom are so deeply rooted in national and religious tradition that they cannot be entirely destroyed so long as the peoples of Eastern Europe retain their national identity.

The history of Eastern Europe provides a wholesome

corrective to the naïve confidence in material progress which was so characteristic of Western culture, alike in Europe and America, during recent generations. It shows us how painful and costly the work of civilization must be: how again and again the Christian peoples have seen their hardly won achievements destroyed in a moment so that they had to start again from the beginning. Yet still the work went on. The ruined towns were rebuilt, the devastated fields were brought back into cultivation and the tradition of Christian culture was kept alive. All this forms an essential part of the common European achievement, since the efforts and sacrifices of the peoples of the East made possible the relative security of the peoples of the West which was the condition of their progress. Thus Eastern and Western Europe are not rival representatives of conflicting traditions of culture. They are members one of the other and owe each other a debt of mutual gratitude and understanding. Professor Halecki's book is a notable contribution to the payment of this debt.

CHRISTOPHER DAWSON

CONTENTS

Introduction

Introduction

In December 1947 I spoke at the annual convention of the American Historical Association on " New Interpretations of Modern European History ". It was the last of a long series of lectures and articles in which during the past twenty-five years I have discussed the problems of the chronological and territorial divisions of history.[1]

My interest in these problems arose from the conviction that this constituted a limited but concrete approach to what is usually called the philosophy of history. As a matter of fact, all the data of history must be systematically organized within clearly defined limits of both time and space before the very content of human evolution can be interpreted in the light of its basic issues. This conviction was formed under the impression of the tremendous changes in international relations which followed the war of 1914–1918. But at present, after the war of 1939–1945, we all feel even more distinctly that our generation is passing from one great period of history to another. The crisis of our times was and is, therefore, my main source of inspiration.

However, before deciding to co-ordinate my ideas and to present them in synthetic form, I was inspired also by two outstanding works which have appeared in recent years. One of them, Arnold J. Toynbee's *Study of History*, is well known, especially since its six big volumes have been condensed in a one-volume edition.[2] It is, therefore, hardly necessary to emphasize its unusual importance and truly universal scope. Gonzague de Reynold's *Formation de l'Europe*—like Toynbee's *Study*, still unfinished—is, as indicated by the title, limited to European history.[3] But since I chose that same starting point, his four volumes proved particularly helpful. And the author's outlook is so universal that he has in fact made a remarkable contribution to the interpretation of history at large.

In both works the divisions of history in time and space, including the problem of Europe's frontiers and constitution, received due attention. But it is perhaps not useless to make these vital and highly controversial questions the object of a special inquiry. The views of a Polish historian now living in America may supplement, in some respects, those of an Englishman and of a Swiss, both of whom have remained in Europe, and contribute to a discussion which will continue for many years.

In its actual form, this contribution is very small. One of the reasons for the brevity of the present work is my desire to avoid any useless repetition of what has already been so well said by others. Furthermore, it has seemed advisable to publish first a preliminary outline, listing the most important problems which still await a definite solution and drafting a programme for further investigations. No single scholar is qualified to answer equally in detail all the questions raised. The writer hopes, however, to return to some of them, which have always been the special field of his research.

In addition to the sections dealing with Central and Eastern Europe, especially in the transition periods from mediaeval to modern and from modern to contemporary history, I should like to develop the ideas sketched in the last chapter. For it is my opinion that the basic problems of international organization which the European Age has tried to solve remain the decisive issues of the world of today and tomorrow. Together with Europe's imperishable cultural achievements, the various plans for the organization of at least one continent, though they issued in failure, survive as an invaluable record of experience for the future generations which will have to organize the world as a whole on the same ageless foundations of national and individual freedom.

CHAPTER I

What is European History?

CHAPTER I

What is European History?

ABOUT fifty years ago a German scholar, Hans Helmolt, created quite a sensation by editing a "world history" entirely different from any other.[1] Its very plan was a reaction against the usual pattern of putting Europe first and following its development through the traditional periods : ancient, mediaeval, and modern. Instead of this, Helmolt invited the various contributors to study the geographical regions of the globe, beginning with America, each one from its origins to the present. He included the so-called "unhistoric" tribes, reached the Mediterranean world not before the fourth volume, and left only the last two, out of eight, for the treatment of Western Europe from the Middle Ages to the present.

In spite of the quantity of new information thus collected, and the new vistas opened, the success and influence of that publication remained somewhat limited. It abandoned the idea of Europe as the centre of universal history without replacing it by any other pivotal conception, and presented so obviously exaggerated a view in the opposite direction that some change of the arrangement had to be made in the second edition. But —what is most important—the European history which nevertheless remained the major part of the whole seemed to be nothing but the sum total of the histories of the various parts of Europe. And that is no adequate definition of European history. Of course, any fragment of the history of any European nation comes under that head, but if we are to understand its real meaning and discover the place which it rightfully occupies in universal history, some other definition must be given.

Let us say, as a preliminary working definition, that European history is the history of all European nations considered as a whole, as a community clearly distinct from any other. Furthermore, it must be admitted that from the moment when Europe was constituted as such a community until the time when its destinies became intimately connected with those of all non-European countries, Europe really occupied a unique place in world history, a place exceptionally important and outstanding.

Such a statement does not mean a return to the old misconception which practically identified European and universal history. Today it would be particularly absurd to defend this, although even now, and even in America, general outlines of what is called world history are more or less histories of Europe, with some information on ancient Egypt and Asia as an introduction and a picture of contemporary global politics as a conclusion. Such an approach, onesided as it is, is based upon the realization that there was a specific period—so long that it might well be called an age—when Europe, as a well-defined unit, really held a central position in the world. This does not at all imply that it was always so, and it obviously no longer is.

The strongest argument in favour of what may seem a privileged treatment of European history is the very origin of the entirely different present situation. It was through European initiative that more or less intimate relations between all parts of the world have been established, with new advantages and opportunities for the non-European parts. The history of that process is a history of European discoveries, expansion, and influence, whatever we may think of their methods and merits. The mere fact that this is so forces the historian to start with Europe if he wants to explain that universal development. It

8

also gives special significance to the apparently remote problem of Europe's own origin, which explains the rise and decline of its power. In other words, the limits, both chronological and territorial, of a European history thus conceived have an unquestionable importance from a universal point of view. And in order to avoid vague generalities, the divisions of European history into chronological periods and geographical regions must be studied with similar care. Europe, if interpreted from the historical point of view, is much more than a geographical unit; it is a supra-national community, and its history is certainly—to use Toynbee's significant expression—" an intelligible field of study ".

It is possible that this great English historian takes too extreme a view when he holds that no history of an individual nation, without excepting his own, can be such an intelligible whole.[2] On the other hand, he admits that even the larger communities, which he calls civilized societies, cease to be completely intelligible in themselves as soon as the problem of " higher religions " is included in the study of history.[3]

But in any case Europe in its historical sense comes nearer than any other community to Toynbee's conception of " an intelligible field of study ", even if we leave open the question whether it comprised one or several civilizations. It is true that it was never completely isolated, as were, for instance, the native societies of the Western hemisphere. But even the continuous relations of neighbourhood with Asiatic societies—civilized or not—are no obstacle to a separate and yet comprehensive study of European history. Such a study cannot exhaust the universal field of world history, but it will always prove the easiest approach to such a general history, especially for those whose own tradition is European, and that means not only the Europeans of today, but also the descendants of those who settled in America, Australia or South Africa.

However, before any detailed analysis is made of historical Europe, it must be repeated that it is—or rather, was—not only a closely knit community, but also an age, which in our day has come to an end. All that has been said about Europe as a field of study intelligible in itself and of primary importance refers only to that European Age. But the very fact that this age is now closed makes the interpretation of European history easier, more instructive, and perhaps also more urgent than before.

It has been frequently stressed that, from the point of view of historical method,[4] ancient history is so instructive to study because it is completed ; we are able to contemplate the whole process of its evolution from the beginning to the end. The same can be said today of European history. That comparison with the ancient, Greco-Roman world is both suggestive and comforting, for it shows that the end of an age, and even of a whole cultural world, need not necessarily mean complete extinction like that which occurred, for instance, in the case of the pre-Columbian civilizations of America. Europe's present decline need not lead to what Oswald Spengler calls an *Untergang*, although the crisis is much more acute today than it was when he wrote his sensational book.[5] Nor need Macaulay's gloomy vision of a New Zealander meditating over the ruins of London[6] ever come true, although this time seemed so near in 1940.

On the contrary : the destruction of the most glorious monuments of Athens and Rome did not mean the death of a civilization to which European culture is more than " affiliated "— to use Toynbee's terminology again. Greco-Roman civilization has survived in its European continuation, and in like manner the latter can survive in the coming age, if again, in spite of substantial changes in geographical limits and forms of organization, the spiritual heritage of the past is preserved—and possibly even enriched and extended.

I. WHAT IS EUROPEAN HISTORY?

In this connection it is important to raise the question of the name of that civilization which Spengler considered doomed. Not only by Spengler, but by a great majority of scholars, as well as in current popular usage, it is called Western rather than European. It is, however, doubtful, whether the former name is really preferable. First of all, " Western " is a purely relative designation which explains nothing—what we call the Near East is western for the Far East, which in turn lies west of America.

But there is an even more serious objection. Those who call European civilization Western are inclined to decide in advance one of the most difficult and controversial questions of European history. They accept the idea of a fundamental dualism in Europe and consider only its western part really European. Gonzague de Reynold makes a basic distinction between two Europes of which only the western one is *l'Europe européenne*.[7] Toynbee does not mention any " European " civilization among the twenty-one civilized societies which he recognizes : besides our Western society, he finds on European soil a distinct Ortho-dox Christian society—in fact, two such societies, one in its original home in South-Eastern Europe and the other outside that region, in Russia, i.e., in North-Eastern Europe.[8]

Since the big issues involved in these distinctions, which can be traced back to the origins of modern historiography, will be discussed in some of the following chapters, only one or two consequences of such an interpretation might be pointed out immediately. First of all, the term Western civilization entails the practical limitation of European history to Western Europe and its leading powers. Even if it is true that in some periods these Western powers played a particularly important rôle, their identification with Europe at large is almost as misleading as the identification of European history with world history. Moreover, if the very name of European civilization is abandoned, an important element which explains the origin and character of that specific form of culture might be disregarded and forgotten.

Although today this so-called Western culture has spread almost all over the world—not without undergoing very considerable transformations—its original European home has obviously influenced it very deeply. Even if we reject the theories of geographical determinism, we cannot completely overlook the close relationship between historical development and the varieties of natural environment, which create conditions and offer possibilities of very different kinds.[9] The conditions which our remote ancestors found in Europe are among the basic factors in the earliest foundations of their culture, and have left permanent traces in the whole course of history.

Even more important than Europe's favourable climate were, in that respect, two other distinctive features of that part of the world. These are its comparative smallness, and, combined with this, the extraordinary variety of particular regions within the narrow limits of that peninsula attached to the huge Asiatic continent. Whatever is colossal and uniform is definitely unEuropean, and that is the secret of all the refinement and distinction of European civilization. It is, too, the profound reason for the importance of small countries, even of city-states, and also for the development of local autonomies, in European history and particularly in the comparative history of individual cultural contributions to a common patrimony.

The variety of the European background is not only geographical, it is also racial, and that disposes of any racial interpretation of European history. There is, indeed, a specific race to which most Europeans belong. But its very name, IndoEuropean, clearly indicates that a large, even the larger, part of that group—a linguistic rather than an anthropological community[10]—settled in Asia and created there, in different conditions, civilizations entirely different from the European.

I. WHAT IS EUROPEAN HISTORY?

The great variety of peoples within the European branch of the " Aryans " has been increased through the complete cultural assimilation of small but not unimportant fragments of other races, even of some of the numerous Asiatic invaders of Europe, the case of the Hungarians being the most striking. And it is hardly less instructive that some of the Finnish tribes became truly European, forming the nations of Finland and Estonia, while others have not to the present day.

The peculiar features of Europe's morphology were nowhere more favourably developed than at the southern tip of the Balkan peninsula, and no other European people succeeded better, nor at an earlier date, in taking advantage of these natural opportunities than did the Greeks. It was therefore in ancient Greece that not only the name, but also the spirit of Europe was born, and G. de Reynold, who calls that country the *Proto-Europe*, has described in some of the most suggestive and original chapters of his work how the tradition of Hellenism contributed to the moulding of Europe's culture until our day.[11]

Whereas de Reynold's study traces with special care the literary aspect of that persistent influence, the work of the Polish philologist Tadeusz Zieliński emphasizes the moral values of Hellenic religion, which in his opinion anticipated to a certain extent the Christian revelation.[12] There is an even more general agreement as to the significance of Greek political thought and practice, which demonstrated more than two thousand years ago that totalitarian government must fail, even under descendants of the heroes of Thermopylae, and that the noblest democratic ideas can be distorted, even by disciples of Pericles, especially when misused for purposes of power politics.[13]

In addition to the instructive examples provided by these experiences in the totalitarian and democratic forms of government, and to the rôle played by Greece in waging against Asiatic imperialism the first fight for the freedom of Europe, the ancient Greeks contributed to the foundation of European history through their experiments in federalism, an element which has been insufficiently appreciated. It was not difficult for Hamilton and Madison to point out the shortcomings of the Achaean League and similar loose confederations;[14] nevertheless they remain the starting point for any serious study of federal government,[15] which is the only system that could have solved Europe's basic political problems.

The Greek and Roman traditions are inseparable in European history, and consequently the whole Greco-Roman civilization is sometimes called simply " Hellenic ", while the whole " Western " civilization is frequently designated as " Latin ". Yet it would seem more exact to say that ancient Rome with its permanent heritage is, in addition to Greek civilization, the second of the mighty cornerstones on which the structure of historic Europe was laid, a second, equally important factor in the development of European humanism, and one which re-appears in each of the successive " renaissances " of European culture.

But it would be misleading to identify the *ordo Romanus*, based on solid principles of law and high ideals of civic virtue, with the *imperium Romanum*, which was neither universal nor permanent, or with the even more precarious *pax Romana*, based upon ruthless conquest. The real greatness of imperial Rome was limited to the brief Augustan age,[16] which was followed by centuries of decline and of Oriental, un-European influence and had been preceded by the centuries of the Roman Republic, which were to have a much stronger appeal for many Europeans of a distant future.[17]

It was not the political unification of subjugated peoples, but the extension of the sphere of a common Greco-Roman culture which was the lasting achievement of the Eternal City. That enlargement of the ancient foundations of Europe was to provide, as is frequently stressed,[18] a truly providential opportunity for the rapid spread of that new, but most important, element of Europe's final constitution which was contributed by Christianity.

Perhaps it was even more providential that the new religion, a *lux ex Oriente* revealed to mankind at holy places far from Europe's limits and soon apparently well established in important Asiatic and African cities, was to find for many centuries its only safe domain, as well as its permanent centre, in Europe. Moreover, Europe and Christendom seemed to become identical ; European civilization was and is often called Christian civilization, and with much better reason than when it is called Western or Latin.[19]

There is a serious danger in that identification, because Christianity cannot be bound to any one tradition or culture,[20] and because, as already pointed out, Europe, even historical Europe, should not be identified with the world which the Gospel is destined to reach. But long before the other continents had heard the Gospel preached for the first time, and after the Near East, including the Holy Land, had been lost to Europe, Christianity penetrated European civilization so deeply that, together with the Greco-Roman heritage which it helped to preserve, it definitely formed the European mind. Even if and when that mind seemed to reject Christian doctrine, it remained more than *naturaliter Christianus* ; it remained faithful, even if unconsciously, to the Christian species of culture. While there had to be, sooner or later, a Christianity outside Europe, there could not be any real Europe outside Christianity. And it was from Europe that the Church set out upon her worldwide mission.

First, however, all the European peoples had to be converted. And it was through that conversion, and no longer through imperial conquest, that Europe's historical limits were extended until they approached the geographical frontiers of the continent. How far that extension proceeded and when it was completed is a vital problem which will be studied below in detail. But it must be emphasized at once that the participation of the former " barbarians " in the formation of Europe was not at all limited to those who crossed the boundaries of the declining Roman Empire. Even more complex and important was the gradual inclusion and co-operation of those peoples who remained in their settlements far beyond these boundaries, in regions of Europe which neither Greek nor Roman influence had hitherto reached.[21]

The general significance of that process does not lie chiefly in the additional territory acquired, nor in the number of peoples who passed from pre-history to history and joined the original nucleus of the European community ; mass and quantity alone never mattered very much in European history. Decisive was the fact that the new members of the European community were and remained different from the old ones and from each other ; in their homelands, and even in the former provinces of the Empire where some of them established their new kingdoms, so many separate nations came into existence as soon as the Greco-Roman civilization in its new Christian expression had been received and adapted to the special needs and characters of the converts.

The result was the formation of a whole series of particular national cultures which together constituted European civilization in its final form. The earlier elements which had contributed to the birth of this civilization, particularly the Christian faith, remained factors of unity. But more decidedly than any geographical compartments, the ethnic and linguistic differences, as well as those of local tradition and mentality, were factors of diversity, almost equally strong. Even within the limits and under the cover of the Roman Empire, that diversity survived Roman rule, which in some cases prepared and promoted the consolidation of tribal groups into real nations.[22] The settlement of all the " barbarian " immigrants and the introduction of all the former " outsiders " into the European society made it finally what it was to be in the following centuries.

Having recalled and briefly defined that fourth and last constituent element of historical Europe, it is now possible for us to implement the preliminary definition given above. Europe is the community of all the nations which, in the favourable conditions of a continent small but full of variety, accepted and developed the heritage of Greco-Roman civilization, transformed and elevated by Christianity, thus giving to the free peoples outside the ancient Empire access to the permanent values of the past.

The history of Europe has now been described with more precision ; but it must still be emphasized that it is not only the history of a distinct community placed in the universal space of the globe ; it is also the history of a specific age within the time of human destinies. Therefore, now that the constituent factors of the European community have been considered, a few words must be said about the place of the European age in the course of the general history of mankind.

It is still customary to divide all history into the three traditional—or, rather, conventional—periods : ancient, mediaeval, and modern. The second-rate German scholar Cellarius, who definitely fixed that division in the seventeenth century (although its elements can be traced to earlier humanistic writings),[23] had an exceptional—and hardly deserved—success with his artificial conception. There has only been added, in recent times, a fourth period, called the contemporary, and gradually it has become obvious that the three original ones can be considered, at best, only as periods of European, not of universal, history. But does even European history, as defined above, fit into that schematic pattern, frequently—and very rightly—criticized, but not yet replaced by any more acceptable division into chronological periods?

Ancient history never was, and could not possibly be, limited to Europe. Even those surveys which are most inclined to identify the world with Europe, and pay little attention to the ancient past of the Far East, start with Egypt and the series of empires in the Near East before turning to the Greeks. It is, therefore, evident that what is usually called ancient history began long before there was any European history, even in the limited sense of the history of any individual people established in geographical Europe. And wherever we may place the beginning of the history of the European community, it is certain that most, if not all, of " ancient " history will remain outside it.

It is equally certain today that most, if not all, of the so-called contemporary period does not belong to the European age. The history of all the European nations is, of course, continuing, but they no longer constitute a community so distinct from all other peoples as to make European history, as hitherto, " an intelligible field of study ", separated as a whole from any other. Nor does the European group of nations now occupy any privileged, leading position in the world.

That great change in the position of Europe is, in fact, the distinctive feature of contemporary history. Therefore, whatever we may think of that purely relative term which necessarily must be abandoned as soon as each new period, in turn, ceases to be " contemporary " for the historians,[24] the events now called contemporary already lead us into another age, an age which follows the European. The chronological boundary between the two is a special question which will be examined later in connection with the problem of the possible survival of European civilization.

I. WHAT IS EUROPEAN HISTORY?

Another question remains to be answered here. Since both ancient and contemporary history are practically outside the European Age—except, perhaps, for the more or less indefinite periods of transition—there remain only two of the conventional periods : mediaeval and modern history. Could we not, then, simply admit that these two well-known periods cover the field of European history, so that no new chronological division of that history is needed ?

There are, however, serious objections to such a simplification of the problem. First of all, the very names " mediaeval " and " modern ", again merely relative terms never intelligible in themselves, would be entirely senseless in such an interpretation. A " middle ages " must be placed in the middle, between two other ages ; it cannot possibly be the first period of any other age. And the centuries of European history that we continue to call " modern " have long ago ceased to deserve that name, which, as a matter of fact, is almost identical with " contemporary ".[25] The German distinction between *neuere* and *neueste Geschichte* is more logical and expressive, but the first of these two terms could hardly be applied to what ought to be considered the last and latest part of the European Age.

But what is much more important than any of the subtleties of terminology is the fact that there is no longer any general agreement as to the limits between mediaeval and modern history. The hesitation of historians between the various dates which are supposed to separate these two periods suggests that a rather long transition period actually intervened. The European Age would therefore include, not the two periods inherited from an erroneous division of universal history, but three periods which should receive entirely new names as soon as their precise limits and their real significance are established.

Before trying to do this, we must realize that the limits themselves—certainly not any individual dates—are less important than the content of each period, which ought to be analysed first. The new division of European history should be based—as in any similar case—upon the main problems of the periods to be distinguished, on problems common to all European nations.

To choose these problems is no easy task, but one by-product of the process will serve as a very useful test : should it prove impossible to apply to the history of any individual nation a chronological division based upon the leading problems common to the rest of Europe, this would be an indication that such a nation, at least in the given period, was not really part of the European community.

It is hardly necessary to emphasize that for even more obvious reasons such a division of European history would have little, if any, significance for the non-European histories of the same centuries. But the European Age as a whole will undoubtedly prove to be one of the main divisions of history at large, since it is the age of European supremacy in the world. And a successful study of the limits of that age, both of its duration and of its area, might be an approach to the philosophy of not only European, but general history.

Already, in the light of these preliminary remarks, a first general observation is in order regarding historical Europe's unity in diversity, which corresponds to a similar unity in diversity typical of geographical Europe, and which is reflected in the character of the most typically European countries : " proto-European " Greece and Switzerland, the " heart of Europe ".[26]

Europe came into existence as an historical community because numerous peoples entirely different from each other, without effacing their particularities and without ever completely uniting politically, joined in a co-operation based upon common cultural conceptions, traditions, and principles. The individual nations which developed within that community were rather small if compared, for instance, with the peoples of India or China. Likewise small was the area in which they had their home ; and compared with the length of other histories—to mention only that of Egypt—the age of their common greatness was of rather short duration.

But within these narrow limits of time we see the same variety of events in rapidly changing periods that is so striking in Europe's physical and ethnical backgrounds. This certainly is an unusually dynamic history, whether proceeding through evolution or through revolutionary upheavals. And that is a first argument in favour of the conviction that the end of the European Age in history is not necessarily the end of Europe, or of a civilization which, though inseparable from the European heritage, has ceased to be exclusively European.

CHAPTER II

The Chronological Limits:
(a) The Beginning of European History

The Chronological Limits:
(a) The Beginning of European History

As THE title of a book which will remain one of the classics of historiography, Christopher Dawson has used a very suggestive expression: "the Making of Europe".[1] One of the main inferences to be drawn from his analysis of this process is that it would be vain to look for the specific date of any year in which the European community came into existence. As a matter of fact, that community was slowly "made" in the course of a long period which, in the light of Dawson's interpretation, covers approximately the whole first millenary of our Christian era.

This is, of course, an approach entirely different from the traditional belief that there was somewhere in the middle of that same millenary a revolutionary change which represents a clear cut between two great periods of history: Antiquity and the Middle Ages. One of the weaknesses of this earlier conception (which still appears in most text-books and in the teaching of history) was and is the uncertainty in determining the event whose date would serve as such a landmark.

Most frequently, however, the year A.D. 476 has been chosen. This was supposed to be the exact date when the Western Empire came to a sudden end ; and while the year 1453, which unquestionably marks the end of the Eastern Empire, has ceased to be most popularly held as the closing date of the Middle Ages, 476 has kept some almost mystical appeal as the date which inaugurated that period. Benedetto Croce tells us the typical story of his schoolmaster who used to say that in 476 the curtain descended on the stage of Ancient history only to rise immediately over the stage of Mediaeval history.[2] We may wonder whether that schoolmaster has definitely disappeared.

Specialists know today that Odoacer's revolution in 476 had not at all that epochal significance which was for long attributed to it. The Polish historian Kazimierz Zakrzewski has proved in an exhaustive monograph that what really happened in that memorable year was not at all a decisive turning point in the history of the Roman Empire, and even less in universal history.[3] And it is by no means fortuitous that this has been shown by a scholar who turned from the study of classical Antiquity to that of Byzantine history, for the progress of Byzantine studies in the last half century has made us realize that the Eastern Empire, always calling itself Roman without any qualification, continued even after 476 to represent the uninterrupted tradition of the Empire as a whole, while the Western Empire, as created by the divisions of the fourth century, had been disintegrating well before 476.[4]

In addition to internal weaknesses which G. Ferrero and M. Rostovtzeff have traced back to the crisis of the third century,[5] that disintegration had as its *causa efficiens* the great migrations which at various moments threatened the very existence of the Empire in the East also. Therefore, even for those who maintain the usual division of history into ancient and mediaeval times, it is now apparent that between these two periods stands, not any single date, but a transition which lasted about three hundred years. Hence " The end of the ancient world and the origins of the Middle Ages "—to quote the title of an outstanding work by Ferdinand Lot, the leading French expert in the history of the " barbarian " invasions[6]— together constitute what is almost a period in itself, corresponding more or less to the centuries of the *Völkerwanderung*.

German historiography, which created the term, used to interpret the consequences of these migrations and invasions of the Empire as a complete break in the Roman tradition which inaugurated a new era : the Middle Ages, as a truly " Germanic " age.[7] It was, however, a German scholar from Austria, Alfons Dopsch, who, as a result of painstaking research which included the whole archaeological background and the cultural and economic aspects of history, explained that there was no caesura, no " catastrophe ", in the development of Europe and its civilization during all the time from Caesar to Charlemagne.[8] What he calls " the foundations of Europe's cultural evolution " is, therefore, like Dawson's " making of Europe ", an uninterrupted process, with no demarcation whatever—either by any individual year, or by the period of the migrations even—between its " ancient " and its " mediaeval " parts. Without carrying the process, as Dawson did, to the end of the tenth century, Dopsch nevertheless preceded the English scholar in breaking with the whole traditional division of history, and approached the origin of Europe from a similar point of view. However, his interpretation, and more particularly the time limits of his study, raises the question whether the foundations of European civilization were not already completed and Europe already " made " in the days of Charlemagne. How difficult it is to answer this question can be seen from a special study made by the Polish mediaevalist Marian Serejski, who tried to find out the real meaning of the name " Europe " when used in the sources of the Carolingian period.[9] And only a few years after the publication of Dopsch's book the great Belgian historian Henri Pirenne started a discussion which must be examined in all its far-reaching implications before any conclusion as to the general problem can be suggested.

In connection with the rather unexpected observation that there is a striking contrast between the Merovingian and the

Carolingian periods, and that the latter was, in spite of a cultural renaissance, a period of economic regression,[10] Pirenne made the even more sensational statement that " without Mohammed there would have been no Charlemagne ". When he developed his idea in a brilliant address at the inauguration of the international congress of historians in Oslo, in 1928, it was found necessary to hold a special discussion meeting in which a dozen historians from various countries raised objections, but at the same time recognized the tremendous importance of Pirenne's hypothesis. After seven years of further research he presented the theory in his last book, published after his death.[11]

In Pirenne's opinion, the end of the ancient world and the rupture of its tradition were brought about in the seventh century by the unexpected Arab expansion which rapidly encircled the Mediterranean from the east, the south, and the west. The centre of Western Christian culture then separated from the Eastern and shifted toward the north, to what were formerly the frontier regions in the centre of the continent ; this led to the rise of Frankish power in the following century, which culminated in the coronation of Charlemagne. That event would thus appear as a consequence of a decisive historical process, which " moved the axis of the world " and proved much more important than the Germanic invasions. The turn from one age to another—being, of course, not connected with any individual date but prepared by a transition of one hundred years (650–750)—would thus occur much later than it would according to the old conceptions, but much earlier than is suggested by either Dopsch or Dawson. Here again, however, the question arises whether that momentous turn really was " the making of Europe ", or only a step, perhaps the decisive one, towards the formation of a new world.

The answer has been facilitated by a side-light of Pirenne's theory, which is more than a problem of terminology such as it may appear at the outset. The facts which he so rightly stressed make us realize that the " unity " which had survived from the fifth to the eighth century, only to be " broken " by the advance of Islam, was the Mediterranean community, [12] and that, in general, the " ancient " world—a relative and almost meaningless term—could, with greater accuracy, be designated as the " Mediterranean " world. We thus arrive at a much more precise idea regarding the age which was followed—or rather, was gradually superseded—by the European Age. And our inquiry as to the beginning of the latter will certainly benefit from a few remarks about the limits and the divisions of the preceding Mediterranean Age.

As a whole, that age and what might be called Mediterranean history is outside the scope of the present study and of its author's competence. It would be especially preposterous to enter here into a discussion of the beginning of that age and the origin of the Mediterranean community. One thing, however, seems unquestionable. This was the first and earliest supranational community to appear in recorded history—and that explains, incidentally, why its history is usually called " ancient," and why the term is comparatively better justified than the designations " mediaeval " and " modern ". But another thing is equally clear. It would be hardly correct to speak of a Mediterranean Age before the various peoples living on or near the shores of the Mediterranean Sea, or at least a considerable part of them, had come into close relations with each other, forming a real community. Their earlier history—or, rather, the little we know about the earliest, quasi-isolated development of each of these peoples—is, of course, already part of " ancient ", but not yet of Mediterranean, history. And this is a first difference between the two terms.

That observation leads immediately to another problem which has more in common with our study of European history, and therefore requires special attention. It concerns the basic character of Mediterranean civilization. No such civilization appears in Toynbee's list of civilized societies, and for good reasons. The Mediterranean community, when definitely constituted, included various civilizations, since the various peoples united in that community had individually achieved a high degree of culture. It is precisely for that reason that we can speak in this case, as in the European case, of a supra-national community, although it might seem anachronistic to speak of " nations " in the contemporary sense when referring to the peoples of so remote a past.

Furthermore, the cultural differences between the various European nations, typical as they are of the European community, are yet much smaller than those between the various members of the Mediterranean community had been. Europe's national cultures have all a common background and cultural tradition. The various cultures which came into existence when, one after the other, the peoples of the Mediterranean region emerged from primitive pre-history could not possibly have anything like that. Toynbee is therefore right if, from his point of view, he considers them all as separate civilizations. For each of them is more of " an intelligible field of study " than any national culture within the European, and particularly within the so-called " Western ", community.

But Toynbee had to recognize, at the same time, the intimate relationship between the different civilizations of the Mediterranean area, including even the society of ancient Egypt, which, though " wholly unrelated "—that is, neither affiliated nor apparented—to any other, did not remain completely isolated. It would prove extremely instructive to add to Toynbee's charts and tables illustrating the relations between civilized societies something like a genealogical tree. Such a tree would show that, with the exception of the civilizations of the Asiatic

II. THE BEGINNING OF EUROPEAN HISTORY

Far East and of the Western, American hemisphere, all civilized societies can be traced back to two or three which originated as close neighbours on the shores of the eastern basin of the Mediterranean, or in its Asiatic hinterland.[13] The members of this small original group of " Mediterranean " cultures and the later societies which are all " affiliated ", directly or indirectly, to one of these civilizations, have so much in common with each other and become so much more " intelligible " when studied in their mutual relations, that it seems justified to speak, on a higher level, of one Mediterranean world.

It is important to note that all the oldest civilizations of that whole region originated around the eastern basin of the Mediterranean Sea, or even further in Asia.[14] Therefore, passing now to the division of the Mediterranean Age into chronological periods, it is not difficult to distinguish two of them : in the first one, the Mediterranean community was limited to that eastern basin only, while in the second period the western basin was included, and the whole Mediterranean Sea became the natural centre of a great historical community, developing in the direction of political and cultural unification.

From the point of view of European history it must be recalled that during the first of these periods, the name of Europe was already invented.[15] Even then that name was used in order to designate a specific part of the Mediterranean lands in contradistinction to the other parts, in Asia and Africa. The relations between the Greek " Proto-Europe " and the nearest parts of Asia—a " Pre-Europe " in G. de Reynold's symbolic terminology[16]—were, however, so close in this period, that in the days of Alexander the Great there was serious danger that the centre of the whole community would move into the Asiatic hinterland of the Mediterranean. If that shift had been effected, Europe would never have been " made ", and there would have been no European Age in universal history.[17]

What really happened, however, was a move in the opposite direction—or, rather, two moves, one from each side—which brought together the eastern and the western parts of the Mediterranean region. Their union was prepared through Phoenician and Greek colonization coming from the East, and finally accomplished through Roman conquest. Even before that conquest included all Mediterranean lands, their history had become an indivisible whole through a process admirably characterized in a famous passage of Polybius, explaining the decisive importance of the first half of the third century B.C.[18] It is therefore possible to point out the specific moment when the second period of the Mediterranean Age began. No similar date can be given with regard to the beginning of the first one, although the description of practically all eastern Mediterranean countries attempted by Herodotus seems to indicate that in his days (towards the middle of the fifth century B.C.) the historical unity of that eastern section was already realized in the consciousness of his generation.

The extension of this community which Polybius described more than two hundred years later seemed to him to cover " almost the whole world ". As a matter of fact, it was only a Mediterranean world which had been " made " as the result of a growing intercourse between various societies which merged their individual civilizations in one Greco-Roman civilization, chiefly Hellenic in culture and politically integrated through the creation of the Roman Empire.

However, the creation of that Empire, which for the Mediterranean world was universal, can be called the beginning of the end of the Mediterranean Age. In this case Toynbee's theory that a universal Empire always appears when any civilized society is disintegrating finds striking confirmation.[19] Even G. de Reynold, who stresses the continuity of the imperial idea in the course of history without quite convincing his reader that this conception of Asiatic origin ever became truly European, has to admit that the Roman Empire was hardly founded when it began to decline.[20]

Yet the moment when Caesar's heritage formally became an Empire under Augustus is not only the beginning of the end of one age—an " end " which was to be protracted for several centuries ; it is also connected with the beginning of what has been called the " making " of Europe and proved to be the introduction to a new age, the European—a process which lasted even longer. Therefore the whole problem of the end of the Mediterranean Age is much more relevant to the object of this study than the other problems of that earlier age, briefly discussed above. It is, in fact, one of the problems directly connected with the time limits of European history, although, after what has been said, it must be admitted in advance that the two ages under discussion were not neatly separated from each other by any single date : the older community was not yet dissolved when the new one was in the making, so that they coexisted during the centuries of a long transition period.

In full agreement with Dawson's interpretation,[21] it must be stressed, first, that the making of Europe started with Caesar's conquest of Gaul. It is very significant that this conquest was completed only about a score of years before the establishment of Roman domination in Egypt. Thus, almost simultaneously, the oldest member of the Mediterranean community was definitely united with all the others in one body politic, and that same state expanded for the first time over a large and important territory lying outside the Mediterranean world. Originally, only the comparatively small part of Gaul situated on the shores of the Mediterranean had been a Roman province, connecting Italy and Spain. Now Rome advanced into the core of the European continent to reach the western and northern maritime limits of Europe, and, before crossing into the

33

adjacent islands, merged all " three parts " of Gaul in one well-defined unit.

That unit was to become one of the main pillars of the European community of the future. Therefore, whatever we may think of the methods of Roman conquest, G. de Reynold is certainly right in emphasizing that Roman rule prepared the formation of the future French nation[22] and contributed to the continuity between the prehistoric Celtic tribes and contemporary France, a continuity which C. Jullian, so critical of the effects of the Roman impact, has outlined from an entirely different point of view.[23]

Neither Britain nor Germany, nor the Danubian countries, were ever completely incorporated with the Roman Empire. It is, therefore, rather artificial to speak of Rome's decisive rôle in the formation of the mediaeval and modern nations which were to appear in these regions, except perhaps in the cases of Switzerland and Belgium.[24] But it is obvious that in the imperial period the *orbis Romanus* consisted of two unequal parts. The main part was indeed the old Mediterranean world, definitely separated from Persia, a world which was neither Asiatic nor African nor European,[25] although it included sections of all three continents. But the Empire also included a considerable non-Mediterranean section of Europe, partly organized into Roman provinces, partly forming a Roman sphere of influence beyond the actual *limes*.

The years in which this was achieved constitute, therefore, a decisive turn in general history, and it is deeply impressive that these were precisely the years immediately preceding and following the birth of Christ. Hence, to speak of a Christian era is more than a question of conventional chronology. In the light of concrete facts, the basic division of all history into two great epochs, B.C. and A.D., appears more convincing than any other.[26]

II. THE BEGINNING OF EUROPEAN HISTORY

Any map of Europe at the beginning of the Christian era, and during the next three or four centuries, shows more or less one half of the continent in colours, corresponding to the territorial divisions of the Roman Empire, while the other half is left white, with only a few geographical and tribal names inscribed. And it is highly instructive to interpret these " two Europes " of a period when the making of the European community had hardly begun.

That basic division has little in common with the future problem of the difference between Western and Eastern Europe. The part of Europe which was already " historic " two thousand years ago included the Balkan peninsula—that is, a large part of Eastern Europe—and did not include, for instance, the Scandinavian countries, which from the very beginning of their history, several centuries later, were considered " Western ". The dividing line was not yet running from the north to the south, but from the north-west to the south-east. That line— which, of course, underwent frequent fluctuations creating transitional zones—separated from each other what we may call Old Europe and New Europe.

Old Europe, under the Roman Empire, actively participated in what is usually considered the last period of ancient history, the centre of historical life still being in the Mediterranean region. New Europe, on the contrary, is little more than a " geographical expression ". It is that part of geographical Europe which was still in the prehistoric age but already on the threshold of history, practically unexplored but occasionally visited by adventurous tradesmen looking for amber on the Baltic shores ; an object of curiosity for some Greco-Roman historians and geographers, who had, however, only the vaguest information on a distant region, the unknown north-eastern limits of which were supposed to be the limits of the world itself.[27]

That division of Europe, though different from any later one, has nevertheless left lasting traces. More important than the archaeological fact that there are ruins of Greco-Roman monuments in Old Europe, which are entirely lacking in New Europe, is the difference of cultural background which even to-day separates parts of the same country situated on different sides of the ancient Roman border. The case of Germany is particularly striking in that respect, but similar observations can be made in Hungary, while in Rumania, whose present territory was only briefly occupied by the Romans, the question to what extent the Roman settlements survived is decisive for the controversial problem of the nation's historical continuity.[28]

There was, indeed, a basic change in the situation when the frontiers of the Empire could no longer be defended, and lost for ever their political significance. For a long time historiography was particularly interested in those " barbarians " who, in the period of the great migrations, crossed these boundaries and settled on imperial soil, first simply penetrating in minor groups into the Greco-Roman world, then invading the Empire in masses, and eventually replacing it, at least in the West, by a number of new, smaller states which were, however, not yet really " national ", but only fragments of the former whole.[29]

Since these states were founded by Germanic tribes, the influence of the " barbarians " who, coming from New Europe, conquered the Old one is usually considered a specifically Germanic contribution to the making of Europe. In the light of Dopsch's theory, mentioned above, that change was not so much a destruction of ancient culture by the Germans as its absorption and continuation by the invaders. And Pirenne has made it clear that, in spite of the political changes which resulted from the Germanic invasions, the Mediterranean community continued to subsist through the centuries of the migrations;

that, as a matter of fact, the migrations did not introduce anything absolutely new in history.[30] It is, therefore, rather more
important, even from the point of view of the rôle of the
Germanic peoples in history, that they not only created states
on formerly Roman territory, but that even those of them who
remained outside the old Roman border were gradually included
in the community of historic Europe. This was another extension of that community far beyond the Mediterranean region,
and it deserves special attention in any study of Europe's
formation.

Thanks to Charlemagne, that extension again took the form
of an extension of the Empire, which, in its new structure,
definitely reached the Elbe, crossed the Danube in the northern,
and followed it in the eastern, direction. But this time it was
more than an advance of the imperial frontier and of what
remained of ancient culture : above all, it was an advance of
Christianity, the most powerful force in the making of Europe
—how powerful it was becomes evident if we consider that
Christianity continued to advance towards the north-east, far
into lands which the restored Empire never succeeded in
absorbing, either under Charlemagne or later under the
German kings. And that leads us back to the initial question
as to when and how the process of Europe's formation can be
considered completed, and which territories and peoples had
to be added to the European community before we can really
speak of the European Age replacing the Mediterranean.

Under the spell of the surviving imperial tradition and of
Charlemagne's personality, it is usually admitted that as soon as
all the Germanic tribes, including the recalcitrant Saxons in
the north-eastern corner, were brought into the restored
Empire, a new age, the so-called mediaeval period, did begin,
with the centre of the new community moved from the Mediterranean towards the north.[31] Even if this were conceded,

the achievement could hardly be called exclusively Germanic. Dawson has stressed the contribution of Celtic Ireland to the making of Europe through the advance of Christianity.[32] And Toynbee has opened new, although highly problematic, vistas by indicating the possibility of the formation of a " Far Western " Christian civilization under Irish leadership, which would have changed the structure of Europe completely had it not, as he says, remained " abortive ".[33]

Both English scholars are well aware of the prominent place which the Normans also occupy in that early phase of European history, particularly in the century following Charlemagne, a place so well described in American historiography by Charles H. Haskins.[34] Long before the three kingdoms of Denmark, Sweden, and Norway were finally organized in their Scandinavian homeland, there was such a radiation of Norman expeditions from Scandinavia towards the most distant regions of the European continent, that Toynbee speaks of an " abortive " Scandinavian civilization which could have contributed to the variety of Europe's cultural development.[35] And one of the states founded by Norman Vikings inaugurated the history of the largest country in Eastern Europe, to which they gave the name of Russia.[36]

This eastern initiative of the Normans, overlooked in Haskins's presentation, has served Dawson as an approach to the problem of how that frontier region, far away from Rome but carefully watched by Byzantium,[37] became a part of the European community. It is, therefore, through a study of both Norman and Byzantine influence on the making of Europe that he came at last to the Slavic peoples, especially to their Eastern branch, which, though politically organized under Norman leadership, soon absorbed its foreign masters, so that the degree of their influence remains the most controversial question of early Russian history.[38] As to the other Slavs, who came into contact with the Greco-Roman world much earlier, they have not yet received sufficient attention in any analysis of the formation of Europe.[39] It is therefore highly gratifying that the Czech scholar F. Dvorník, after publishing important contributions to the study of the relations of the Slavs with both Rome and Byzantium in the ninth century, is now preparing a book on " the making of Central Europe " which will fill a gap in Dawson's work.[40]

It took the whole second half of the first Christian millenary before all Slavic peoples had entered the European community. Their Southern branch settled during the sixth and seventh centuries in large regions of the Eastern Empire, and later, following the example of the Slavicized Bulgarians, created new states in the invaded territories,[41] just as the German tribes had done, some hundred years before in the lands of the Western Empire. The two processes, ending in the Christianization of the invaders, are therefore analogous and complementary, in spite of differences which will be examined later.

The Western branch of the Slavs, separated from the former through the Magyar conquest of the Danubian plain, which around 905 destroyed the Moravian state—incorrectly called an Empire—entered into relations with the Empire of Charlemagne in the ninth, and with that of the Ottonians in the tenth, century. In the case of the Czechs this contact resulted in both Christianization and inclusion in the Empire. The Slavic tribes between Elbe and Oder, opposing both Christianity and German domination, had lost any chances of survival before the European community was completely formed.[42] The Poles, who thus became Germany's immediate neighbours, were converted in 966 through the intermediary of Bohemia, but, unlike Bohemia, they succeeded in creating a completely independent state.[43] The date of 1000, when the independence of Poland was recognized by Emperor Otto III at the congress of Gniezno,[44] can be considered, in agreement with Dawson's conclusions, the final date of the making of Europe. For in the next year newly converted Hungary received from the pope the royal crown which was to remain her national symbol; a few years earlier, in 988, Kievan Russia had officially received the Christian faith from Byzantium; and at about the same time, conversion to Christianity made the three Scandinavian kingdoms full-fledged members of the European community.

The conception of that community represented by the well-known contemporary picture which shows Otto III on the imperial throne, receiving the homage of *Roma*, *Gallia*, *Germania*, and *Sclavinia*, remained a dream of the young Emperor, who died in 1002 without having succeeded either in extending his influence as far as Kiev or in settling German-Polish relations by having a king of Poland as the Empire's collaborator in the Slavic world.[45] But the inclusion of that whole world in the Christian community which Rome and Byzantium, not yet definitely separated from each other, continued to lead was an extension of that community equal in importance to the earlier inclusion of the Germanic world. And with only the small group of Baltic peoples still outside—but already the object of missionary activity[46]—most of geographical Europe and almost all the peoples of the European race were at last united in one civilized society, the variety of which only increased its vitality.

The tremendous north-eastern extension of Christian Europe during the ninth and tenth centuries was at the same time a badly needed compensation, because in the two preceding centuries Christendom had lost to Islam almost all of its Asiatic and all of its African territories, and even, temporarily, the Iberian peninsula. The Arab invasion not only destroyed what still remained of the Mediterranean community, but made the ancient " Roman " sea—once the centre of a civilized world —a frontier between two civilizations.[47]

The epochal significance of that fact has been well brought out by Pirenne. But he seems to go too far when he tries to prove that the Muslim onslaught, endangering the communication lines through the Mediterranean, definitely separated the Byzantine East from the Roman West,[48] thus making possible the re-establishment of a separate Western Empire. Actually, the close relations between the old and the new Rome, whether friendly or hostile, did not cease ; Byzantium, entering the most heroic, truly epic period of its history,[49] continued to defend Christendom, long before the Western crusaders, in the borderlands and outposts of Asia Minor and Syria ; and the Western Empire, only temporarily restored by Charlemagne, was not really reconstituted before the second half—962—of the tenth century, which still belongs to the millenary of Europe's slow formation.

The Mediterranean Age ended, after at least four hundred years of decline, in the course of the eighth century. Two hundred years later, the European community, prepared since the beginning of the Christian era and compensated for the losses south of the Mediterranean by the gains in North-Eastern Europe, entered the time of its greatness : the European Age.

CHAPTER III

The Chronological Limits:
(b) The End of European History

CHAPTER III

The Chronological Limits:
(b) The End of European History

IN HIS foreword to Eric Fischer's provocative book on " the passing of the European Age ", Sidney B. Fay remarks that the work itself is " not quite so pessimistic as the title suggests ".[1] Now, whereas Fischer does indeed reach the conclusion that, though " the Age of European Western Civilization is gone . . . transformed Western civilization may survive in new centres outside Europe ",[2] it nevertheless seems evident that he is going too far. It is an exaggeration to compare the " passing " of European civilization with the complete disappearance of the cultures of the Incas or the Mexicans.[3] And in spite of the shifts, transfers and transformations of Western civilization which he so ably describes, there is no reason for predicting that this civilization, in its renewed form, will survive only on other continents.

It is certainly true that our civilization, together with all the others which still exist in the contemporary world, is passing through a crisis which can be rightly compared with the crisis of Greco-Roman civilization towards the end of the Mediterranean Age. But Toynbee's qualified optimism, expressed in his comparative study of civilized societies, is based upon an observation which makes us distinguish civilizations which are totally extinct from those which survive in what he calls " affiliated " societies.[4] Furthermore, such an affiliation might be very loose, so that the historian remains rather doubtful about the whole connection, or, in other cases, so close and intimate that it is entirely obvious.

Such is precisely the case in the relationship between the " Hellenic " and the two Christian civilizations, Western and Eastern, which appear on Toynbee's list, or between the Mediterranean and the European Age, to use the terminology of the present study. That terminology proves helpful when we turn to the problem of the possible relationship between our " passing " civilization and that which will follow—or, rather, is now in the making. For the geographical terms Mediterranean and European clearly indicate that though there was a shift of cultural centres, involving territorial losses and gains, a fairly large part of the territory, the European sector of the Mediterranean world, remained the same, greatly contributing to the continuity between the two ages and their civilizations.

However, before studying that territorial problem, which requires an investigation of the geographical limits of European history, it is necessary to continue the study of its chronological limits. And now that we have examined the dates of the " making of Europe ", we must seek similar dates for what a pessimist might call the " un-making " of Europe, and what undoubtedly is the end of a whole age. In doing so we must, of course, always remember that, whether we study the beginning or the end of such an age, it will never be identified with the date of any individual year, but with a transition period which may last for centuries, and during which the two ages, the declining and the rising, seem to coexist. Such was the situation during a large part of the first millenary of our Christian era, and, in spite of the accelerated rhythm of modern and contemporary history, we have to expect something similar towards the end of the second millenary.

This great process of gradual change need not necessarily involve the " passing " of Europe as a whole. If we call it the end of European history, this certainly does not mean that there will not be, in the future, a European history in the sense in which such a history developed early in the Mediterranean Age. But it will again be chiefly the history of individual European countries, or of certain parts of Europe within larger, not exclusively European, communities. The European community typical of the European Age of history, a real unity in all its diversity, a unity clearly distinct from any other part of the world and occupying in the world at large a truly unique position, temporarily a position of leadership—that community will no longer exist. It is disintegrating before our very eyes.

In order to grasp the full implications of this change, and to answer the question as to when the process of disintegration started, let us examine the characteristics of the European community at the height of its historical rôle.

First of all, it is well to remember that throughout the whole course of European history in its proper sense Europe was practically identical with Christendom. From the decisive years around 1000 almost all European peoples, but only these peoples, were united in the same Christian faith. The last European heathens were converted in the following centuries,[5] while outside Europe only a few Christian communities, most of them separated from the main body of the Church, survived after the Mohammedan conquest.[6]

Around the same time, the survival of the Greco-Roman culture, renewed before and after 1000 in a whole series of renaissances,[7] was assured in the European part of the Mediterranean world, and the heritage of that culture transmitted, together with Christianity, to all the other parts of Europe. Thus both traditions, Greco-Roman and Christian, were intimately associated on European soil, and the two elements combined in the formation of a specifically European mind which contained great potentialities for development.

47

It is true that the early dreams of a harmonious state system, uniting Europe politically as it was united in faith and culture, did not come true. But even after the failure of mediaeval universalism there appeared, one after the other, various plans for an organization of Europe.[8] Invariably such plans were limited to Europe alone, often in opposition to non-European forces ; and usually they were influenced by the belief that the European community, identical with the Christian Republic and with " real " culture, actually *was* the world, or at least its natural centre.

There was indeed, within the European community, a great variety of cultures. That diversity resulted from geographical conditions, from differences in the ethnical background, from a great variety of vernacular languages—which never ceased to be used, in spite of the tremendous rôle of the common classical languages—and, eventually, from an ever-increasing difference of national consciousness. Around the year 1000, the various European nations of the future were already in formation, and therefore the roots of European nationalism, though its " vogue " did not come before the nineteenth century,[9] must be traced back far into the Middle Ages.[10] But these cultural differences never were as profound as those which before the Roman conquest, and even under the cover of Roman domination and the spread of Hellenism, had separated the various civilized societies of the Mediterranean world. Furthermore, these differences within the European world were almost insignificant if compared with the cultural cleavage between Christian Europeans and non-Christian non-Europeans.

There was, therefore, a European solidarity, not always strong enough to overcome the endless rivalries between European nations, nor even to organize the common defence of Christian civilization, but manifesting itself in the crusading spirit which survived the fall of Acre[11] and maintaining, until the end of the European Age, a feeling of superiority on the part of Christian Europeans in relation to other cultures, religions, and races. Whether justified or not, that feeling could not but result in a claim to supremacy in the political and economic fields also.

This same sense of superiority resulted in that identification of European history with universal history which amounted to more than a biased approach on the part of those who wrote history, since it was reflected in the actions of those who made history. In the earlier centuries of the European Age, this can be explained by the fact that most of the other parts of the world were virtually unknown and isolated from Europe. Later, in the times of discovery and colonization, it was to a large extent a question of prejudice and conceit. But it has already been pointed out above[12] that, except in the cases of the Asiatic invasions of European territories, the contacts of the European community with other civilized societies, as well as those with tribes on a genuinely inferior level of culture, were a result of European initiative and usually issued in European conquest and domination. And it is also true that no other civilization included such a variety of national cultures, nor represented a religious conception of similar universality. To what extent Christianity has been misused by those whose armed force or economic exploitation preceded, followed, or even accompanied, truly missionary activities is, unfortunately, another question.

This leads us to the main question of how and when it became at last apparent that Europe, in spite of its real greatness, was *not* the world, and how and when Europe lost its position of leadership. The roots of a gradual process of disintegration can be traced back far into the past of the European Age, just as in the case of any other declining civilization, particularly in that of the Mediterranean world. There was, however, in the European case, a widely spread illusion which concealed the

49

danger for a long time. That illusion was the almost naïve faith in an uninterrupted progress of what was usually called Western culture.

There was, indeed, such a continuous, increasingly rapid progress in the field of material culture, especially after the so-called " industrial revolution ", which was neither a real revolution in the sense of a sudden, violent change of existing conditions nor a revolution limited to industry,[13] but a long series of technical improvements and scientific inventions applied to practical needs that gradually transformed the European Age into something like a machine age.[14] That mechanical progress, which increased the quantity of production far more than it perfected its quality, was by no means an unqualified blessing. Better than any other writer, Henri Bergson has described the truly tragic discrepancy between the extraordinary extension of the field of action in which the human body can exercise its physical power, and the unchanged limitations of our minds and souls.[15] And today, whenever the problem of progress is discussed, the conclusion is that our " tremendous material progress has not been accompanied by any corresponding advance in other fields ".[16] The European generation which seemed to have reached the height of perfection in practical achievements has rightly been called " a generation of materialism ",[17] and only those who accepted the materialistic philosophy invented in the lifetime of the preceding generation could be satisfied by what was such an obvious break with the European tradition.

But long before the last *fin de siècle*, and even before the generation of Karl Marx, there were definite signs that the transition period from the European Age to quite another age of history had set in—or, at least, was approaching. These signs might be studied first in the highest sphere of life, the religious.

Christianity was so typical of, and so intimately associated with, European civilization, that in the earlier part of the European Age, the so-called Middle Ages, Church and culture had been inseparable.[18] In the thirteenth century—which, from this point of view, can be considered the greatest of all[19]— the *philosophia perennis* seemed to have established a lasting harmony, not only between faith and reason, but also between the two fundamental constituents of the European mind, the Christian and the humanist traditions. But one of the successive revivals of the latter, the one to which the name of Renaissance has remained specifically attached, opposed these two elements to each other. The attempts to create a culture which would be European without being Christian were initiated by the neo-pagan wing of the humanists[20] and resumed under the slogan of " enlightenment ". And their apparent triumph in the secular-ization of nineteenth-century culture is now recognized as the main cause of the present crisis of European civilization.[21]

At the same time Christianity, abandoned by so many Euro-pean leaders and divided by others, who wanted to reform the Church, into rival denominations, developed an extraordinary missionary activity outside Europe. This activity, which ac-companied Europe's colonial expansion, redeemed the dark sides of that colonization and compensated Christianity for its setbacks in Europe. But after so many Christian settlements had been made on other continents and extended by the con-version of millions of natives, the identification of a religion spread all over the world, in obedience to Christ's command to His disciples, with one part of the world, in which many millions remained Christian only nominally, was becoming more and more unjustified.

Voltaire hoped that the European community which was no longer the *Respublica Christiana*, would nevertheless remain a " Great Republic ", organized on the basis of the balance of power system.[22] But that seemingly realistic idea proved no less utopian than the dreams of the French pacifists of that century and the preceding one.[23] And this leads us to another reason for the passing of the European Age. The making of Europe took a whole millenary. The next millenary was occupied by the task of organizing Europe, but there was a complete failure to establish a *Pax Europaea*, even as a temporary illusion corresponding to the illusory *Pax Romana* towards the end of the Mediterranean Age.

Toynbee would say that this is just a proof that Western civilization is not yet passing, because the universal state which appears as the last phase of all civilized societies has not yet united ours.[24] After all the failures to create such a universal state on European soil—the failure of mediaeval universalism as well as those of modern conquerors in the Napoleonic style[25] —it now seems probable that such a state will never appear. The diversity of Europe proved stronger than its unity. Coming after countless other wars, some of which had involved most of the countries of Europe, the war of 1914–18, the greatest and last " European War ", had such consequences that European civilization obviously could not stand another. When, nevertheless, such a war started in 1939, it necessarily became a real World War, decided by non-European forces and ending in catastrophe for the whole of Europe.

This World War also put an end to the old idea of European leadership in the world. But that idea, too, another typical feature of the European Age, had started to vanish long before. In order to be more than an illusion of pride, such leadership required a real European solidarity, a solidarity such as had already been violated when, instead of joining in the defence of Christendom against the Ottoman onslaught, leading European powers co-operated against others with the common enemy of Christendom.[26]

It was an illusion that colonial imperialism would lead to a real domination on the part of Europe beyond the seas. The only result was an endless rivalry between the colonial powers which no papal arbitration could check, either in the days of Alexander VI or in those of Leo XIII. Moreover, there was a violent reaction against European control, among both the dependent native populations and the colonists themselves. When the tottering Ottoman Empire was admitted in 1856 to the European concert, and when, a little later, the United States and Japan were recognized as " big powers " in addition to the six nations which, at the given moment, happened to be the strongest in Europe,[27] it was clear that world leadership was no longer a European privilege.

The European community could no longer raise such a claim because its internal unity had been destroyed, not only by international, but also by civil wars. These revolutions were, of course, primarily directed against a given form of national government, but usually they also questioned and threatened at least some elements of the general European tradition and of its normal evolution. The period of particularly frequent, violent, and widespread revolutionary movements in Europe which started with the French Revolution of 1789 reached its climax in the totalitarian revolutions of the twentieth century.[28] At least two of them had in common a total rejection of both the Christian and the humanist tradition. Since Nazism originated in the very centre of Europe and almost achieved the conquest of the whole continent, its victory would have meant the total destruction of European civilization. Communism, having been established in a border region of Europe and in the adjacent part of Asia, immediately raised the question as to how large a part of geographical Europe would be lost to the cultural and historical European community and become part of Eurasia. And that is precisely the sign of Europe's

53

final disintegration as well as the crucial problem of our time.

The analogy with the final disintegration of the Mediterranean community through the loss of wide territories to the world of Islam is, of course, striking. And that comparison raises another question : whether such a loss to the European community would be similarly compensated by an expansion in the opposite direction, creating a new community, not through a total destruction of the existing civilization nor through a complete break with its tradition, but through a shift of its centre. The question is not difficult to answer : long before the European Age had passed, European culture had spread over a whole continent beyond the Atlantic, and created such a close cultural community between the countries on both sides of that ocean, that Toynbee does not, as in other similar cases, distinguish the offshoot from the main body of the civilized society, which he continues simply to call " Western ". Furthermore, the provocative political discussions of Walter Lippmann[29] and the penetrating historical interpretations of Ross Hoffman[30] have suggested, and gained acceptance for, the most convenient name of the new unit, which they call " the Atlantic community ".

Developing the comparison between the two transition periods, it must be stressed that, just as the making of Europe started long before the Mediterranean Age had ended, so the origin of the Atlantic community can be traced back to events which preceded the passing of the European Age.

By far the most important of these events was, of course, the discovery of America, which was immediately followed by a gradual process of conquest and colonization.[31] It is true that this was part of a much larger, really world-wide process of European expansion. But on no other continent did the Europeans discover enormous territories so favourable to their permanent settlement. In no other part of the world were the natives, comparatively few in their number, so completely subjugated. The conquest, effected partly through warfare, in which the native population was greatly reduced, and partly through a process of absorption, was so complete that no traces remained of their civilized societies and political organizations where these had existed. And, finally, to no other overseas region did European colonists come in such vast numbers. A long and uninterrupted flow of immigration from practically all countries of the Old World, not only from the lands on the Atlantic shores,[32] had made a new Europe in America before the old Europe passed.

It is no exaggeration to call the Western hemisphere, as a whole, a New Europe, just as a small part of the original English colonies is still called New England and many American cities received an old European name with the addition of the word " new ". For the entire heritage of European culture, which included its well-preserved heritage of Mediterranean, Greco-Roman civilization and the whole Christian tradition in the form of all the different denominations, was brought to the other side of the Atlantic.

European civilization found on the new continent fresh possibilities of development, from which it produced a new type, a new variety, of the common patrimony, thus increasing the diversity which had characterized European culture within the boundaries of the continent of Europe. When that differentiation had progressed sufficiently to create a new way of life and a new form of government—though one based upon the political philosophy of European Christendom[33]—the Americas claimed their political independence, just as any European country would have done in similar conditions.

The Declaration of Independence and the writing of the Constitution of the United States, the creation of the twenty

Latin-American republics, and the transformation of Canada into a self-governing Dominion were all further steps, not only in the making of America, but also in the formation of the Atlantic community. For a real community could not consist of independent states on one side of the Atlantic and dependent colonies on the other side, and the destinies of all the countries in New Europe proved inseparable, in war and peace, from those of their former mother-countries.

Another step in the same direction was made when one of the American republics became strong enough to be considered a Great Power equal to those of Europe. The United States had by then expanded to the Pacific, as had Canada, and that is important to remember because, in connection with the fact that several Spanish-American countries are situated exclusively on the Pacific coast, it clearly shows that membership in the Atlantic community is not limited to countries on the Atlantic shores, the Atlantic Ocean being only the geographical centre of a much wider region.

The Spanish War, fought both in the Atlantic and the Pacific, was the first test of that new position of the United States. Twenty years later the new Great Power was able to play a decisive rôle, through its armed interference, in the last great war which was mainly a European war, and to initiate an international organization, which proved necessary since all attempts to organize Europe separately—including the last one, the so-called European Concert—had ultimately failed. After a last withdrawal into an illusionary isolationism outside the League of Nations, America's even greater rôle in the Second World War and its membership in the United Nations appear as the climax of a development which started in 1492, with 1776 as the decisive turning point, almost coinciding with the beginning of Europe's great revolutionary crisis.

III. THE END OF EUROPEAN HISTORY

These obvious facts are so impressive that there is a danger of two equally misleading interpretations, which would give to " the passing of Europe " an exaggerated significance. The first of these appears in the book with precisely that title published by Eric Fischer. In his opinion, not only is Europe's leadership —political, economic, and even cultural—a thing of the past, but so also is " Western civilization in Europe ". And even if " the rise of new centres need not spell decline for the old ", even though Europe may not " succumb " completely in the present crisis, the shift of centres of gravity means, not only a " transportation ", but a " dislocation " which involves an " inner transformation " and leaves only a " modest future " to European cultural centres.[34]

Now it is certainly true that, transferred to other continents and particularly to the Western hemisphere, the old civilization of Europe is undergoing changes of such extent that the cultural differences between the two continents—though not those between Anglo-Saxon culture in North America and in Britain—are greater than those between the various European nations. But in spite of all the kinds of " Pan-American " co-operation which have created a continental organization never achieved in Europe, it would be hard to decide whether Latin America has closer ties with North America than with the Iberian peninsula ; and, quite recently, distinguished American historians have rightly emphasized the unity existing between the American and the European parts of one common civilization. In his brilliant presidential address before the American Historical Society, Carlton Hayes has shown that the frontier of that civilization on the European continent is at present a new frontier of America, while " the Republic's old frontier, completing its westward march, has disappeared from the American continent ".[35] And Garrett Mattingly wants American educators to realize that " our history is western history, moved by the same rhythms, stirred by the same impulses, inescapably involved in the same crises " as European history.[36]

Although the Atlantic Age has only started, it is already apparent that it will have more in common with the European Age than the latter had with the Mediterranean Age. To use Toynbee's terminology, this would mean that the affiliation between the two civilized societies which succeed each other is much closer in the present case than it was between what the English historian calls the Hellenic and Western civilizations. For him it is even more than affiliation : it is identity of civilization in Western Europe and America.

Without going as far as that, it must be pointed out that there really is such an identity at least in the religious sphere, with even the surviving natives of the Western hemisphere converted to Christianity ; that there is in America an increasing interest in the mediaeval tradition[37]—i.e., in that phase of European culture which preceded the discovery of America ; and that in the " melting pot " of the United States—not to discuss here the special case of the French Canadians—the various ethnic groups, all equally good American citizens, are rightly proud of their specific European heritage, which in each case is a valuable contribution to America's full development. There is much more space in the Western hemisphere than within the old, narrow limits of Europe, and that difference in size and proportion is certainly one of the reasons why the diversity in unity is less conspicuous on the western side of the Atlantic than on the eastern. It remains, nevertheless, one of the many distinctive features which the whole Atlantic community has inherited from the European.

The American part of that new community—a compensation for the territories lost in Europe through the Communist revolution—is by far the larger in area, though not in population. It also is today by far the richer one, and one of the

American republics emerged from the Second World War as the world's strongest power. But that does not necessarily mean that Europe's own rôle has ended, that its impoverished and partly destroyed cultural centres will not be restored to their former greatness, nor that the younger, but rapidly growing centres beyond the Atlantic will represent an entirely transformed civilization.

In spite of a variety of national and regional cultures greater than ever before, and in spite of hitherto unknown geographical distances, reduced through new facilities of communication, there is in the Atlantic community, as now definitely constituted, a solidarity at least equal to the historical solidarity of the European nations. And only in common can the peoples of common origin on both sides of the Atlantic—the Mediterranean Ocean of a new age—continue to exercise a leadership in the world, justified not by their material power, but by the high spiritual values which they defend.

Precisely because of the spiritual character of the Atlantic community, a few more nations of the same origin and cultural background can share that solidarity in spite of their geographical isolation. This refers, of course, to the distant members of the British Commonwealth which are neither European nor American : to South Africa, which has, indeed, an Atlantic shore, but is separated from the other members of the community by a whole alien continent of unknown future, and also to Australia and New Zealand on the other side of the globe.

But that observation leads us directly to a much larger issue, and at the same time to the second possible misinterpretation of the passing of the European Age. When he speaks of new centres of culture which seem to have better prospects than the old ones in Europe, Eric Fischer is thinking not only of the Western hemisphere, but of all continents ; and, on the other hand, he speaks of an Americanization not only of Europe, but of the world.[38] Similarly, in Toynbee's opinion Western civilization, common to Western Europe and America, is the only civilized society which is not yet disintegrating, and it has consummated, through its world-wide expansion, " a single Great Society ", although it is by no means the only component of a unified world in which it might be gradually relegated to a rather modest place.[39] And in the ever closer relations of all lands in war and in peace the idea of "one world" which Wendell Willkie's book has made so popular[40] seems to be realized.

Should we not, therefore, say that the European community is being replaced, not by the Atlantic or any other geographically limited community, but by a global unity which would lead us into a world age with a common, truly universal history?

There is undoubtedly a progressive unification of the world in the sphere of economics, communications and even political relationship, as evidenced in the United Nations Organization. But that does not necessarily mean that the world is equally unified in the much more important sphere of ideas and culture. For the purely material assimilation of the various cultures, which we call Westernization or Americanization, there is no corresponding spiritual unity; such unity as there is remains limited to those who share the common tradition of Christendom, including the heritage of Greco-Roman humanism. This is precisely the reason why it is so difficult to make the whole world accept our conception of democracy, based upon that very tradition; why intellectual co-operation must not be based upon a non-existent common philosophy of all mankind;[41] and why not only two or three " worlds ",[42] with different political ideologies, but several more, separated by basic cultural differences, are going to co-exist with the Atlantic community in the next age of human evolution.

We are entitled to speak of that next age as the Atlantic Age, just as the preceding one was rightly called European, because the Atlantic community, composed of America and a large part of Europe, seems to inherit the central, leading position in the world which Europe occupied before. But without deciding in advance that problem of the future, without speculating about the possibility, nor the desirability, of a universal " World Age " which might follow in later centuries, without even discussing with Toynbee the number of the other civilized societies which will continue to develop outside ours, let us conclude with some chronological precisions with regard to the " passing " from the European to the Atlantic Age.

The Atlantic community began before the European ended, and therefore, just as in the case of the Mediterranean and the European communities, both coexisted during a transition period. This time, however, owing to the accelerated rhythm of history, the period was considerably shorter ; instead of covering a thousand years, comparable to the millennium of Europe's making, the new transition, only foreshadowed in the so-called age of discoveries, did not really begin before the American Revolution, and ended with the last war.

This time the continuity which, in spite of an even more striking shift of the centre of gravity, links the two communities succeeding each other is much closer, were it only because of the uninterrupted and unchanged religious tradition. Moreover, this time the new community was practically made before the older one had really passed away. But though a large part of the European community is surviving as part of the Atlantic one, European history, in the sense in which it corresponded to the millennium of the European Age—from the middle of the tenth to the middle of the twentieth century—has come to an end. There now remains first, to study the geographical limits of what had been its field, and then to investigate its geographical divisions, which might indicate the narrower limits of the part to be taken over by the Atlantic community.

CHAPTER IV

The Geographical Limits:
(a) Oceans, Seas, Islands, and Straits

CHAPTER IV

The Geographical Limits:
(a) Oceans, Seas, Islands, and Straits

IT HAS become a commonplace to say that Europe is nothing but a peninsula of Asia. This over-simplified definition creates the impression that Europe's limits must be easy to define. But even from the merely geographical point of view such an impression is misleading. And the difficulty appears much greater if we try to study the frontiers, not of Europe as a geographical unit, but of the European community and of its history. For, on the one hand, the area of historical Europe was more than once considerably reduced through invasions and temporary conquests by non-European peoples, while, on the other hand, the European nations, after reaching the geographical limits of the continent, crossed them through various processes of colonization.

Moreover, whatever our approach may be—purely geographical or historical—at least one frontier of Europe remains obviously undetermined and controversial. This is, of course, the limit in the East, where the European peninsula is attached to the Asiatic continent, not through any narrow isthmus like those which connect Asia and Africa or the two Americas, but through a wide stretch of land where natural boundaries are not easy to discover. However, before touching this most important basic problem, it must be pointed out that, even in the three other directions where maritime shores seem to fix such natural boundaries of Europe without any possible doubt, the course of history has not always been determined by these limits.

There are various reasons which explain this unexpected difficulty of interpretation. First of all, even seas, and sometimes even oceans, are not unsurmountable barriers, separating once for all the peoples living on opposite coasts. Much depends on the progress of navigation, which may create ever closer ties between territories apparently separated by maritime frontiers. This is particularly striking in the case of the so-called " mediterranean " seas, and it so happened that some of these seas—including the most typical, to which the name Mediterranean became specifically attached—are precisely in the European region.

Furthermore, the European continent is surrounded in various directions by islands, great and small, which played an unusually important historical rôle. The connection of these islands with the mainland was not always equally close, and sometimes the policy of their inhabitants seemed to connect them more intimately with non-European territories.

Last, but not least, in some places the sea which separates Europe from other continents becomes so narrow that the resulting straits, far from being real divisions, are permanent links between their bordering shores. They create the possibility of easy passage from and to Europe, and in no other places have there been more territorial controversies in history. The crossing of these gateways from either side has increased or reduced for centuries the area of the European community, with both sides of the straits under the control of the same European or non-European power.

If, after these general considerations, we begin a survey of the maritime boundaries of Europe, we find the simplest situation in the north. For the Arctic Ocean, undoubtedly a barrier, and not a way of communication, is one of the final limits, not only of Europe but of the habitable world, with only the pole, a purely mathematical point, beyond it—or, rather, in the middle of it.

It is almost symbolic that the pole, which for so many years had been the goal of thrilling adventures, full of romantic appeal[1] but without any real historical significance, was eventually reached towards the very end of the European Age. For in the following periods the possibility of flying over the whole polar region may change the situation altogether.

In the course of European history, the main problem was not so much the exploration of the arctic world and its islands as the extension of permanent settlements and political organization as far as the coast of the Arctic Ocean, and the developof a regular navigation along its shores. The famous Chancellor expedition of 1553[2] was certainly a turning point in that respect, definitely extending the field of European history as far as the Archangel region. It is true that, long before, the colonization of this extreme north-east of geographical Europe had contributed to the wealth and power of Novgorod,[3] while the conquest of that whole Republic, in 1478, had made Moscow a great power and given to Russia complete security from the north.[4] A similar security from that side was a permanent factor in Scandinavian history, explaining, to a certain extent, the rôle of the Normans in the Middle Ages and Swedish imperialism in modern times, although otherwise the sparsely populated lands of the Lapps hardly contributed to the historical development of either Sweden or Norway.

All three Scandinavian kingdoms receive too little attention in the usual presentation of European history, and " the voice of Norway ", which had no period of great-power expansion but constituted from the start " a living link " in the Atlantic system,[5] was almost silenced during the period of more than five hundred years in which Norway was connected either with Denmark or Sweden. The latter countries had the advantage of being situated, not on the somewhat isolated north-western border of Europe, but on the Baltic Sea, which is rightly called another Mediterranean.

This analogy, instructive as it is, should not be overstressed. The Baltic never really was a frontier of the European community. But it remained the most accessible gateway to some countries which were included in that community later than most of the others. It was also the centre of a limited, regional community with its special balance-of-power problem : the struggle for the *dominium maris Baltici*.[6] In that problem of a rather distant frontier region, most European powers were involved, directly or indirectly, being at least affected by the issue whether the entrance to the Baltic should be closed or open. Since these straits led through the wide-open North Sea to the Atlantic Ocean, all the countries on the Atlantic shores had a special, though not always sufficiently realized, interest in a sea which, as a matter of fact, is nothing but an isolated bay of the Atlantic. In past centuries, when Denmark controlled both sides of the passage between the Baltic and the North Sea, this resulted in a powerful position for that small country.[7] Today it ought to be evident that all the Baltic countries, including those on the eastern coast, are an integral part of any real Atlantic community.[8]

If the Baltic never became a Scandinavian lake, it was because of Scandinavia's divided interests. Attracted by the ocean on their western borders, the Scandinavians were the first to cross it in times of extremely difficult communications. Of the two large islands which served as steppingstones in that earliest passage to America, Iceland, though an " Ultima Thule " far from Europe's coast, became definitely European ; and, in spite of unfavourable climatic conditions, this early centre of truly European, typically democratic culture has survived, with a parliament which recently celebrated its millennial anniversary.[9] The challenge of environment proved too strong in the case of Greenland, and the first, abortive discovery of the Western hemisphere only shows one of the possibilities of what Toynbee calls the " abortive " Scandinavian civilization.[10]

As mentioned before, Toynbee also speaks of an abortive " far-Western " civilization with its centre in Ireland.[11] Yet, in this instance, as in the other one, the prospect which remained unrealized was probably not the creation of a separate civilized society, but that of a leading rôle in the European community. In each case, one of the obstacles was the peripheral position of the region which made such a promising start. In the case of Ireland, there was also conquest by a foreign power, coming soon after the outstanding contribution which that " island of saints " had made to the very formation of Europe. Ireland's fate during the latter part of the European Age was, in turn, a cause of the prominent part played by the Irish people in the making of a new community on both sides of the Atlantic.[12] But at the turn between the two ages, liberated Eire resumed her rightful place among the nations of Europe.

This Ireland started as a free member of a Commonwealth created by the neighbour island of Britain. And if the country of St. Patrick was always an integral part of Europe, the same must certainly be said of the country of Shakespeare. All projects for organizing Europe without Britain were, and are, doomed in advance.[13] The Channel never has been, and could not be, a frontier of Europe ; and this is even more true in the historical than in the geographical sense. Of course England's colonial expansion beyond the seas went farther beyond Europe's limits than any other process of colonization, but all these processes are typical of European history, of its greatest as well as of its worst features. Even as the centre of a world-wide Empire, Britain did not cease to belong to Europe, but only prepared the transition from the European to the Atlantic Age. And when, in the British Commonwealth, the ties between its constituent parts became so much looser than in the old Empire,[14] the United Kingdom itself returned to an association with the rest of Europe closer than in the days of British imperialism.

All the islands in the north-west of Europe were, from beginning to end, pillars of the European community, and since they were advance posts in the Atlantic Ocean, they are now also pillars and connecting links in the Atlantic community.

What has been said about Britain is equally true with regard to the countries situated along the western shores of the European continent. For them, too, the Atlantic Ocean did not prove to be a limit to expansion. They all had, and to some extent still have, large colonial empires—much larger than their European territories. Yet it is precisely thanks to these homelands at the maritime border of Europe that the countries in question all had a prominent place in a history which was in fact European history, to which the histories of colonial wars or colonial trade were merely appendices.

Even in the case of countries as small as Holland and Belgium, it is evidenced by the famous historians which they produced, by men like J. Huizinga or Henri Pirenne,[15] that their constructive contribution to the development of the European community was without proportion to their limited area. And as for France, one never thinks of this great nation as one formed at the extreme western end of the continent ; historically, France was in the very centre of Europe, not only a cornerstone of the European state system but a fountainhead of all trends of culture throughout the European Age, the leader in any joint action of the European community, from the Crusades[16] to the spread of modern democracy in what has been called a " French Europe ".[17]

Why, then, is it that, turning to the Iberian peninsula, we enter countries which, in spite of their great and uninterrupted

Catholic tradition, seem to be less European ? Even in Portugal, so typically an Atlantic nation, the most sympathetic observer recognizes a certain non-European impact.[18] The same is true of the proud charm of Spain.[19] What has been said concerning all the other colonial powers suffices to prove that this difference was not the price to be paid for a glorious rôle in the age of discoveries. But some of the finest monuments of architecture survive, to suggest the obvious origin of these non-European features : the Arab conquest.

Not only is the Iberian peninsula geographically close to Africa, with merely a narrow passage between them, but it was through Northern Africa that this European border region was invaded, when Europe was still in the making, by Asiatic conquerors with a completely alien civilization. Brilliant as it was in many respects,[20] that foreign culture, supported by a well-organized foreign domination which in the south of Spain lasted almost eight centuries, temporarily included the whole peninsula in the Muslim world. Gradually the " reconquista " moved Europe's frontier again southward, from the Pyrenees, where Roland and his knights had defended it, to the walls of Granada, which resisted until the discovery of America. But even the violent reaction against any possible Moorish danger which followed, and the special devotion of Spain and Portugal to the mediaeval Christian heritage, were insufficient to obliterate the fact that, throughout the Middle Ages, part of their territory, though geographically European, had been outside the limits of European history.[21]

These limits were never constituted by the Straits of Gibraltar, which the Ancients rightly considered not so much a frontier between two continents as a gate from the well-known Mediterranean to the unknown Atlantic world.[22] Long before they had become, in modern times, a passage between two equally well-known regions, and even before the last Muslim strongholds in Spain were retaken, the Straits were crossed by the advancing Christians : with the struggle for Ceuta, which Calderon made immortal,[23] begin the fascinating pages of European history which concern the southern coast of the Mediterranean. And that raises the big question as to what extent the Mediterranean Sea ever really was a frontier of historical Europe.[24]

The tradition of the ancient, Greco-Roman world, very much alive throughout the European Age, kept all Europeans conscious of the fact that during an earlier and even longer period the Mediterranean, far from being any sort of barrier, had been the centre of all the surrounding lands, including large parts of Africa and Asia. Moreover, not only at the Straits in the West, just mentioned, and those in the East, to be discussed later, but also in its very centre, the Mediterranean Sea was easy to cross, thanks to a chain of islands, large and small, which, in spite of the temporary withdrawals of Europe, always remained closely associated with her. In any case, that long bay of the Atlantic seemed much less of an obstacle than the ocean itself, which was, however, crossed by Europe's expansion. Yet the complete reconquest of the non-European parts of what had been, until Mohammed, the Mediterranean community proved to be a task beyond the forces of the new European community.

As a matter of fact, there had usually been, even in antiquity, a rivalry between the countries north and south of the Mediterranean ; in the case of Rome and Carthage it led to a deadly hostility.[25] Even under Justinian, the Byzantine Empire exhausted its forces in the effort to reunite all the Mediterranean lands, including North Africa, [26] which, less than two hundred years later, was so rapidly overrun by the Arabs as to be completely cut off from Europe. The Crusaders failed whenever they attempted to attack either Tunis or Egypt, even if a city like Alexandria was temporarily taken, [27] and while the Ottoman

Empire soon after the conquest of Egypt reached the frontier of Morocco, Charles V had to withdraw from before Algiers.[28]

It is true that France was more successful three centuries later, and even made precisely that colony an integral part of the Republic, with French protectorates east and west of it. But in our times it has proved impossible for Italy to follow the footsteps of ancient Rome in Libya, and for Britain to keep Egypt under her control.

So it would seem that it was and is a hopeless undertaking to revive the idea of a Mediterranean community in order to associate with Europe any larger part of Africa. It was from other coasts that European powers succeeded in penetrating deep into the African continent, until they had divided most of it among themselves. And far from making it a part of the European community—with the sole exception of the most distant south—they converted it into a typically colonial, sometimes ruthlessly exploited, area. African history, whether old as in Ethiopia or young as in Liberia, though strongly influenced by European power politics and, in the case of the latter country, even by the United States of America,[29] hardly became at any moment a part of European history, nor a preparation for inclusion in the Atlantic community. The strategical interests of Europe in Tangier and of America in Dakkar cannot change a picture determined by the complete difference of the whole cultural background.

To return to the Mediterranean, which, after all, became in the course of so many centuries more of a frontier than the Sahara, this sea remained, however, a sphere of European initiative. And if we may speak of a balance of power between the incompatible worlds of Europe and Africa, the preponderance was almost regularly on the side of the smaller continent, where, for two thousand years, a " concentration of civilized power has been developed ". The Hungarian statesman who recently used that expression rightly pointed out that only thanks to such " a co-operative Europe " north of the Mediterranean could that sea, Europe's southern limit, serve in modern history as the life-line of a Great Britain situated on the other side of the continent.[30]

For the same reason, all the important Mediterranean islands, some of which served as links in that line, have remained almost constantly under European control. Even at the height of their power the Arabs could not keep Sicily. Even Suleiman the Magnificent, who started his lifelong " Mediterranean adventure " by taking Rhodes, eventually failed before unconquerable Malta.[31] It cost the Turks a war of almost twenty-five years' duration to take from declining Venice the island of Crete,[32] which remained a centre of opposition until its liberation. And the history of Cyprus, from the crusades of the Lusignans to the tragic death of Bragadino[33] (or rather, from the England of Richard the Lion-Hearted to the Britain of Disraeli and Gladstone), is hardly less significant.

It is even more significant if we consider the situation of this island, in the extreme north-eastern corner of the Mediterranean, near the Asiatic coasts of Anatolia and Syria. Here we are very far from that eminently European centre of the Mediterranean world which was and is immortal Italy, a peninsula which, prolonged by the islands of Sicily and Malta, clearly divides that sea into two basins. The eastern basin had always been a great battlefield between Europe and Asia, with the Adriatic bay as Europe's last line of defence—a fact which will prove important for the problem of the divisions of European history. It was here that Europe, in the time of the great offensive Crusades—the *passagia ultramarina*—made its farthest advance, temporarily retaking almost the whole Asiatic part of the ancient Mediterranean community. But it was here, too, that Asia found the most convenient passage for invading

Europe by crossing those Straits which proved so crucial in all history that they became *the* Straits *par excellence*, no special name being needed for their identification.

These Straits never seemed to be a limit, nor a way into the unknown, like those at the western end of the Mediterranean. They were crossed as often as the passage between Asia and Africa, where an isthmus only recently converted into a canal made communication so much easier. Long before the problem of the Straits became connected (sometimes even identified) with the question of freedom of navigation between the Aegean and the Black Sea—apparently an internal question of the Concert of Powers of modern Europe—it was one of the main issues in the ancient struggle between Europe and Asia. Therefore the usual approach of studying the Straits controversy only from the later part of the eighteenth century[34] is misleading ; and from a truly universal point of view the story ought to begin at least with the legendary siege of Troy, if not with the rôle of Aegean civilization and of Asia Minor as something like a " Pre-Europe ".

Without discussing here the latter conception, so important in G. de Reynold's interpretation of Europe's origin,[35] it must be pointed out that this specifically Asiatic peninsula occupies a prominent place not only in the history of the Mediterranean community, to which Asia Minor undoubtedly belonged, but also in the history of the European Age.

Asia Minor was most intimately connected with that other " Asiatic peninsula "—Europe—as long as it remained part of the Eastern Roman Empire, that symbol of the continuity between the Mediterranean and the European Ages. Not only the coasts of Asia Minor, inseparable from the traditions of ancient Greece, but the whole peninsula constituted the main basis of Byzantine wealth and power. Charles Diehl, otherwise particularly interested in Byzantium's relations with the West, has often stressed this decisive fact,[36] and another distinguished Byzantinist, Henri Grégoire, in studying the Byzantine epics,[37] had the best occasion to show that the most heroic and inspiring fights in defence of the frontiers of the Empire were conducted for many years in the border region where the Anatolian peninsula is attached to the continent of Asia.

Does this mean that in those early years of the European community that small peninsula had closer ties with the larger, European one than with Asia proper? This is probably true, but it could not possibly result in the definite inclusion of Asia Minor in historical Europe, because as early as the eleventh century, the first century which fully belongs to the European Age, most of Anatolia was conquered by the Seldshuk Turks, and it was never completely reconquered.[38] It is, however, significant that its partial reoccupation by the Greeks was, in spite of so many mutual disagreements, one of the main results of the First Crusade, and that after the Fourth, which turned against Constantinople, the Byzantine Empire survived on the Asiatic side of the Straits,[39] with another Greek Empire established in far away Trebizond,[40] in the north-eastern part of Asia Minor.

Another wave of Turkish conquests was needed to decide the struggle for Asia Minor in favour of Asia, and for a short time the Straits really were the limit between Asia and Europe, not only geographically but also politically and culturally. But hardly had the Ottoman Turks occupied, in the first quarter of the fourteenth century, almost all Greek possessions east of the Straits, when, in the middle of the same century—to be exact, in 1354[41]—they crossed the Hellespont and took their first stronghold on European soil, the strategic key position of Gallipoli. Retaken by the Christians only for a few years, [42] Gallipoli was to be the starting point of the gradual conquest of the Balkan peninsula and the encirclement of Constantinople. The fall of the imperial city, imminent at the end of the fourteenth century but delayed by the Ottoman defeat in the battle of Angora (1402) against another Asiatic conqueror Tamerlane, became unavoidable when the Crusaders of 1444 failed in a last attempt to cut off Asia Minor from Europe by naval forces sent to the Straits.[43] From 1453 on, both sides of that narrow passage remained in the hands of the Ottoman Empire.

These well-known facts raise the question of the very character of the Ottoman Empire. The great Rumanian historian N. Iorga, although himself belonging to one of those Balkan nations which suffered cruelly from the Turkish onslaught, admits that the Ottoman Empire was a continuation of the Byzantine, whose place it simply had taken.[44] Toynbee goes even further, considering the Turkish and not the Greek Empire to be the " universal state " of the Orthodox Christian society.[45] Both interpretations would lead to the conclusion that, established on European soil, the state of the Osmanlis became part of the European community. Its system of government, which used as one great slave-household of the Sultan the most gifted children of all Christian subjects, taken from their families and converted to the Moslim faith, is praised in A. H. Lybyer's frequently quoted book as the most efficient and remarkable " ruling institution " in Europe,[46] and suggested to Toynbee the idea of a special civilization created by the Osmanlis, which, had it not been " arrested " by the decline of their Empire, would have taken its place among the civilized societies of the European continent.[47]

With all respect to these prominent scholars, it must be observed that their conclusions seem strangely paradoxical. Modern Turkish historiography rightly stresses the basic differences between the Byzantine and the Ottoman Empires.[48] And from the European point of view it must be observed that the Ottoman Empire, completely alien to its European subjects in origin, tradition, and religion, far from integrating them in a new type of culture, brought them nothing but a degrading foreign domination which interrupted for approximately four hundred years their participation in European history.

During these centuries the European frontier of the Ottoman Empire, a typically Asiatic state expanding even more rapidly in Asia and Africa,[49] was the south-eastern limit of the European community and of its history, even when Turkish victories had pushed far into the heart of geographical Europe. In his brilliant outline of European history, Henri Pirenne has correctly interpreted that process as a major catastrophe for Europe.[50] Coming later and lasting longer than the Arab conquest of the Iberian peninsula, the Ottoman conquest of the Balkan peninsula is the obvious reason why that very region where Europe originated seemed so different from the happier parts of the continent when, at last, it was liberated.

For the same reason, there was no problem of the Straits as long as they were in the very centre of an Empire equally strong on both sides to control the passage completely. The situation changed when the reconquest of the Balkans by Christian Europe approached the Straits, which this time seemed to become a real frontier of Europe, both natural and historical. But at the same time the rôle of the Straits as a gateway between the Mediterranean and the Black Sea became more important than ever before, since a new great power emerged north of the latter sea, looking for an outlet to the former. It was then, near the end of the eighteenth century, that the Straits problem, the crucial issue of the Eastern Question in its modern sense, changed its aspect, while remaining basic for both European and Asiatic history.

The rivalry among the reconstituted Balkan States and practically all the great powers of Europe made it impossible for any European nation to reach the Straits by occupying Constantinople. Therefore, in spite of the Turkish defeats between 1912 and 1918, the imperial city remained in their hands, no longer as their capital—which was removed to Asia Minor—but as a bridge-head of Asia on European soil, similar to the mediaeval bridge-head of Europe in Asia Minor. The last traces of that latter bridge-head disappeared with the exchange of populations after the Lausanne treaty of 1923, which was chiefly a transfer of the Greeks of Asia Minor to Greece proper.[51]

Thus at the very end of the European Age the limit of the European community at the south-eastern corner of Europe coincided with the geographical, maritime frontier between Europe and Asia Minor, but with the important exceptions of Constantinople and the European coast of the Straits. The fact that this whole region, after the failure of the projects for its complete internationalization,[52] was left to Turkey did not hinder a real reconciliation between that new Turkey, a national state with no imperialistic aims beyond its Anatolian territory, and the former victims of Ottoman conquest.[53] If the Straits remained a danger spot in international relations, it is in connection with the problem of the last and most controversial sector of Europe's frontiers : its long land frontier in the north-east.

However, before that sector is studied in a separate chapter, a few words must be said about the isolated bay of the Mediterranean, beyond the gate of the Straits, which is called the Black Sea. For that sea, too, is undoubtedly a frontier region between Europe and Asia, well known to the ancients, with almost all its coasts included in the Mediterranean community, but reduced to a secondary rôle in the European Age, especially in the times when it was practically a Turkish lake.

Before the establishment of Ottoman control, direct or at least indirect as in the Khanate of the Crimea, the Greek colonization of the Pontic region had been followed by a colonial expansion of Genoa and Venice which made even distant trade centres like Caffa in the Crimea, or Tana at the mouth of the Don, outposts of the Western world.[54] These influences did not, however, penetrate far into the hinterland of those ports, and in 1475 the fall of Caffa, after a few years of a Polish protectorate, put an end to such developments.[55] It was only three hundred years later that Russia took the place of Turkey, first on the northern shores of the Black Sea and then in the whole region of that sea, except for its definitely Asiatic part, the northern coast of Anatolia, where the Greek Empire of Trebizond had disappeared eight years after the fall of Constantinople.

But which part of the Pontic region was really European? Without returning to the problem of the Balkan peninsula, only temporarily severed from historic Europe through the Ottoman conquest, it is easy to realize that the answer to this question, as far as the territories north of the Black Sea are concerned, depends on the solution of the bigger problem as to how far the European community reached in the east of the continent. Since obviously it never extended as far as the south-eastern corner of the Black Sea, two countries of ancient traditions and entailing, in each case, relations with the Greco-Roman world and a heritage of Christian culture, remained in dangerously isolated positions outside the European world; these are Georgia[56] and, even closer to the Asiatic mainland, Armenia.[57] The tragic histories of those two nations certainly affected Europe both at the beginning of the European Age, when the Seldshuk conquest of Armenia resulted in a western emigration of many of her people, and at the end, when Georgia and possibly even Armenia seemed to have a chance for real freedom, supported by the sympathy of Western Europe and America.[58] Nevertheless, hardly ever was the destiny of either of these nations an integral part of European history.

The Mediterranean, with its frequently ignored Pontic extension, has thus led us once more outside Europe. Perhaps it is not, therefore, altogether surprising that, at the end of the European Age, not this comparatively narrow sea, but the wide Atlantic Ocean itself, has ceased to be a real and durable limit of Europe. Turning more and more towards America, which was first touched upon at the beginning of the European Age, discovered in the middle, and emancipated near the end, Europe was able to liberate her southern peninsulas from foreign invasions, colonize Africa and fight Asia at the Straits, but the Mediterranean lifeline remained a borderline parallel to the icy Arctic Ocean in the north.

The European part of what is developing into the Atlantic community thus extended from one sea to another—*a mari usque ad mare*, as the inscription at the entrance of the Mediterranean University Centre at Nice reads. But would all of Europe join the Americas in the new Atlantic Age? No answer to that vital question can be given without studying the line which running from the northern to the southern maritime border of Europe, constitutes her eastern limit somewhere on the large isthmus which connects the European peninsula with its North Asiatic background.

CHAPTER V

The Geographical Limits:
(b) The Great Eastern Isthmus

The Geographical Limits:
(b) The Great Eastern Isthmus

ON PTOLEMY's famous map of the ancient world,[1] drafted at a moment when the making of Europe had only begun and the Mediterranean community had reached the highest degree of unity, the unknown wilderness north of the Black Sea and of the Greek colonies on its coast is called Sarmatia. The Father of Geography knew little more about that legendary land than had the Father of History who, six hundred years before, called it Scythia. But Ptolemy could realize much more clearly than Herodotus, whose conception of Europe was necessarily vague,[2] that in this north-eastern region the limit between Europe and Asia was much more difficult to determine than at the familiar place where the Straits seemed to separate them quite definitely. He hesitated to include the whole of Sarmatia in either Europe or Asia, and distinguished between *Sarmatia Europea* and *Sarmatia Asiatica*, with the Don, a river which he called the Tanaïs, as the frontier between them.

Fourteen centuries later, among the scholars of the Renaissance, the same conception prevailed,[3] not only because they were in this case, as in so many others, influenced by the ancients and their terminology, but also because in the meantime, in spite of so many changes in Europe's evolution, it had not become easier to find a more adequate boundary. The only trouble was that the rather arbitrary dividing line of the Don had no continuation through the northern part of the Sarmatian plain to the Arctic coast, just opened to trade relations with Western Europe.[4]

Here in the north-east Russian colonization had already approached the Ural mountains, but it rapidly crossed them, to reach the Pacific after no more than sixty years.[5] Russia's " urge to the sea ", which had entailed a long, hard struggle in every other direction, attained its goal in the Far East with a rapidity which can only be compared with the advance of the American frontier to the opposite coast of that same Pacific three hundred years later.[6]

There is, however, a tremendous difference between these two frontier problems. In America a federal union, created on the eastern shores of the continent, expanded as far as its western shores. But the whole area, whether on the Atlantic or the Pacific, became one United States of America. In the so-called Old World, an empire that had originated on European soil proceeded to occupy the whole north of Asia ; but the territory acquired through that colonial expansion certainly did not become part of Europe, even though the colonization was not of overseas territories but of an adjacent, contiguous area. Even in the days when the Russian Empire was a leading member of the European Concert, a clear distinction used to be made between European and Asiatic Russia, though that administrative boundary did not quite coincide with what is now commonly considered the geographical frontier between the two continents.

As far as that geographical dividing line is concerned, its most uncontroversial sector is, of course, the range of the Urals. But even these mountains, of moderate height and with easy passages, have never been a real barrier between the wide plains of similar character on both sides.[7] Farther to the south there is a gap of at least four hundred miles between the end of that chain and the Caspian Sea, where the Ural river is even less of a real, natural frontier ; on the contrary, it is precisely that open gate which was used from time immemorial until the days of Tamerlane, at the end of the fourteenth century, by a long series of Asiatic invaders who at least temporarily overran and conquered large parts of geographical Europe.[8]

Furthermore, if the eastern boundary of Europe is supposed to reach the Caspian Sea, another sector of the frontier between Europe and Asia must be discovered on the isthmus between that large Asiatic lake and the Black Sea. Here geography offers two possible divisions :[9] the Manych depression, more to the north, or the high wall of the Caucasus, farther to the south. But the first of these divisions would be purely morphological, without any historical significance, and it so happened that remote centres of ancient Christian culture developed not north but south of the Caucasus.[10]

These Trans-Caucasian regions, definitely in geographical Asia, were considered under the last Tsars to be part of European Russia, whose administrative boundaries did not even follow the Ural mountains or the Ural river, and in several places were arbitrarily extended beyond that hardly conspicuous line. There is, accordingly, no reason whatever why the historian should pay any attention to it.

The approach of the historian to this problem must, in fact, be entirely different. Since a purely geographical solution is obviously inadequate, and since it is equally obvious that the area included in the historical concept of the European community cannot be extended indefinitely into the plains of Northern Asia, the question arises whether the eastern frontier of that community ever did reach the Urals, whether it did not, in fact, remain west of it, as in Ptolemy's interpretation. And that question, in turn, introduces the major problem of the relationship between Russia and Europe, a problem which T. G. Masaryk, in his penetrating study of the Russian mind,[11] has rightly considered the crucial issue. It is, indeed, of decisive importance both for the understanding of the largest country on the European continent and for any study of the limits of European history.

Which part, if any, of Russia was part of historical Europe and its cultural community ? To raise that delicate question, which involves two others regarding the possible divisions of Russia and the time limits of her participation in the European Age, is not unfair to the Russians. For, with all its implications, it has been asked, and continues to be asked, by the Russians themselves, particularly by their greatest spiritual leaders, and by their best friends, among whom T. G. Masaryk undoubtedly belonged.

In Masaryk's standard work, as well as in all similar studies of Russian culture and the origins of modern Russia, whether written by a Russian such as Paul Milyukov[12] or by a foreign scholar such as Jan Kucharzewski,[13] who is the leading Polish specialist in that field, the traditional distinction between the two main schools of Russian thought, the Westerners and the Slavophils, is clearly apparent, although foreign observers are more aware of what both schools have in common. Today it is, however, equally apparent that a third school, only touched upon by scholars whose chief interest was in the nineteenth century, has become of similar importance : the Eurasians.

Only the Westerners would answer (as could be anticipated from their very name) that the whole of Russia was always part of the historical European community, except that her association with the West was not equally close in all periods owing to certain factors which delayed Russia's development. In their opinion, Russia never was basically different from the rest of Europe ; the only difference to be admitted, even in consideration of the nineteenth-century " Europeanization " of Russia, is explained by the fact that, in some respects, Russia

88

still *was*, at that time, what Europe had been before.[14] According to this view, Europe's historical boundaries would coincide more or less with the geographical, both being constituted by the eastern frontiers of the European part of the Russian Empire, whose Asiatic part is a colonial area comparable to the overseas possessions of any other European power.

The Eurasian school represents exactly the opposite point of view. Its ideology is far from homogeneous,[15] and that is only natural, since it originated under the last Tsar, was developed later by Rightist émigrés, and at the same time seemed to correspond more closely than any other to the conception held by the Soviet Union. But it is definitely a strong belief in Russia, or the Soviet Union, or the federal Eurasian Empire of the future, as a world in itself, a sub-continent which belongs neither to Europe nor to Asia, although it might be considered a link between the two. The basic difference from Europe and the importance of the " Turanian " element are particularly emphasized, while the difference between the European and Asiatic parts of the totalitarian Empire vanishes completely. The obvious conclusion is that the eastern frontier of the European community always was and is the western frontier of Russia.

Although various aspects of the Eurasian doctrine still require much discussion and investigation, the conclusion itself, so important for our present purpose, is clear and simple. The same could not be said with regard to the conclusions of the Slavophil interpretation of Russia, which certainly deserves special attention. Nobody has shown more clearly than Michael Karpovich that there was among the Slavophils an evolution from a well-justified interest in, or even enthusiasm for, Russia's cultural background, to a political, aggressive nationalism on ethnic grounds.[16] And while the former could find its place in a general European tradition, common in spite of its diversity, the latter opposed Russia to the " rotten " West in a feeling of superiority which excluded any real community with the rest of Europe. Furthermore, even an isolated, deeply critical thinker like Chaadayev, who, far from being proud of Russia's difference from any other country, feared that she had taken the worst elements out of these foreign cultures, could not but come to the same conclusion, that Russia was not really part of Europe.[17]

Whether optimistic or pessimistic, that conclusion, combined with an almost mystical belief in Russia's specifically Slavic character, had far-reaching implications concerning all the Slavs. Independently of the political consequences of a Panslavism which, in its Russian interpretation, was to lead to an absorption of " all Slavic rivers in the Russian ocean ",[18] the conviction that the greatest, the leading Slavic nation was different from Europe as a whole was naturally extended to all the other Slavs, opposing the so-called Slavic World to a Europe identified with its Western part alone.

Strangely enough, these extreme conclusions of Russian nationalism, intensified by Panslavic imperialism, which seem to lead *ad absurdum* any historical interpretation of Europe as a whole, were in practical agreement with an equally onesided Western approach dictated by an equally conceited feeling of superiority with regard to all the Slavs and to a few smaller nations geographically and historically associated with them. Karamzin was just completing his life work glorifying the uniqueness of the Russian state as superior even to the Roman Empire,[19] when F. v. Ranke declared in the introduction to his first important book[20] that the European community was limited to the Germanic and Romance nations. In the Prussian school of German historiography that conception had a distinctly anti-Slavic character, even if, in the study of the modern period, an exception was made regarding the traditionally allied Russian

Empire.[21]   Another exception, in favour of the Catholic nations east of Germany[22], which could hardly be excluded from the " Christian Republic ", remained rather theoretical, since not only German, but also Anglo-Saxon and sometimes even French historiography neglected such nations until recently in their general conception of the European community.

But even the exclusion of Orthodox nations merely because of their religion is obviously unjustified. The strongest argument against such an interpretation of historical Europe is the case of Greece : it was here that Europe's history had its beginning, and the glorious tradition of Hellenism inspired a modern national revival,[23] and yet that same country became the centre of Orthodoxy, inseparable from the other Balkan countries which she so deeply influenced. Were it only for that reason, S. H. Cross is right in pointing out that it was *not* that Greek influence which cut Russia off from Western Europe.[24] The Byzantine impact was strongest in the Kievan period of ancient *Ruś*—Russia in its original sense, whose name has no counterpart in any Western language—and yet it is precisely that part of Russia and that period of her past which most certainly must be placed within the limits of European history.

The formation of the Kievan state, whatever might be said of the relations between the basic Slavic element and the Norman stimulus, both European, was an important step in the " making of Europe ", as discussed above.[25] F. Dvorník's recent research shows the intimate connection of Kievan Russia with the West.[26] The Eastern Slavs united in the Kievan state entered the European community soon after the Western Slavs and before the final break between the Western and Eastern Churches, the Cerularian schism, whose consequences did not appear in Kiev until at least sixty years after its consummation in Byzantium.[27]

But what about the following phases in the evolution of Russia ? This name has today a meaning entirely different from that of the old *Ruś*, since it became the designation of only part of the Eastern Slavs, more specifically called the Great Russians, and of the state which they created around a new historical centre. It is that geographical difference between the basin of the Volga and those of the Dnieper and the Dvina which must be stressed even more than the ethnic and linguistic differences which resulted in the formation of three East Slavic nations. For throughout the Middle Ages those of the Great Russians who, together with the two other groups—now called Ukrainians and White Russians—remained in the original home of all Eastern Slavs, remained at the same time in particularly close association with Europe ; the history of Novgorod and Pskov, until the Muscovite conquest, has a special significance in that respect.[28]

What changed the situation long before any national differences within the old *Ruś* became apparent was the colonial expansion of some Great Russian tribes towards the northeast. That colonization started almost as early as the Kievan state itself,[29] and in the twelfth century had definitely created a new Russia " beyond the forests ". A recent celebration has recalled that the future centre of this new Russia, Moscow, the " pivot of an Eurasian Empire ",[30] is mentioned for the first time in 1147, although it was, at that time, still in the shadow of the earlier princely residences in Suzdal, Rostov, Vladimir, etc.

Did this colonial Russia of Suzdal and other places become part of the European community, since it was, after all, part of geographical Europe in the usual interpretation, different in this respect from that other and much larger area in Asia which Moscow was to colonize a few hundred years later ? It cannot be said in advance that such a Europeanization of the

Volga region would not have been possible as an immediate consequence of the settlement of so many Slavic colonists with their Christian Churches and under their princes, all belonging to various lines of the old Kievan dynasty, which had concluded numerous matrimonial alliances with the ruling families of Europe.[31] There were, however, from the outset serious obstacles to any real assimilation of that vast region, distant from all centres of European culture, including Byzantium. To the difficulties resulting from the completely different racial background, represented by the native population of pagan Finnish tribes, there must be added at least the political opposition between the two Russias, old and new, evidenced in the destruction of Kiev by forces from Suzdal as early as in 1169,[32] and also the different form of government, of a purely autocratic character, which was developed in unusually hard and primitive conditions of life.[33] But what proved decisive was something else : the unforeseen catastrophe of the Mongol invasion in the thirteenth century.

That this was a real catastrophe from the general European point of view has been clearly recognized by the greatest Western historians from Ranke to Pirenne,[34] who have compared it with the Ottoman conquest of the Balkans. Here again it was a conquest, not necessarily by " barbarians "—though the Tartars were on a cultural level inferior to that of the Turks —but nevertheless by invaders completely alien in all spheres of civilization, to begin with religion. Therefore S. H. Cross is again correct when he contrasts that Asiatic domination " which left an indelible imprint on the Russian character "[35] with the influence of Byzantium's brilliant Christian and European culture, and when he sees in the former, and not in the latter, the powerful factor which cut Russia off from Europe. Almost all Russia, old and new, with the sole exception of the Novgorod region, was now part of a gigantic Eurasian empire whose western limits were, of course, the eastern boundaries of what remained of Europe.

The Mongol domination of Russia was of shorter duration than the Ottoman rule in the Balkans, but it was forced upon the Russians when they were at an earlier stage of cultural development within the European community ; even Kievan Russia had entered it only two hundred and fifty years before, while the new, colonial Russia of the Volga region had not yet been integrated in that community at all. And it was precisely in this north-eastern region, where the first prince of Moscow appeared just a few years after the coming of the Tartars,[36] that their overlordship was to last the longest—about another two hundred and fifty years—and the influence of Saraï (the capital of the geographically European part of the Mongol Empire, near the site of present-day Stalingrad) was to be the closest and deepest.

That anti-European influence never reached a similar degree of intensity in the original, truly European part of Russia ; especially is this true of her south-western border region, where, immediately after the catastrophe of 1240, first the metropolitan of Kiev[37] and, a little later, Prince Daniel of Halich and Volhynia entered negotiations with Pope Innocent IV, which led to a temporary religious reunion.[38] Crowned king by the pope's legate in 1253, Daniel planned to co-operate against the Mongol danger with Catholic Poland and with Lithuania, which was also temporarily under a Catholic king. That promising scheme failed, but, as a matter of fact, the issue was only postponed : in " Little Russia ", as Daniel's heritage was called, his last descendants, who perished fighting the Tartars, were succeeded by Polish rulers, and, at the same time, the so-called White Russia and the Ukraine were liberated from Tartar domination by Lithuania.[39]

The word " liberation ", so frequently misused, is appropriate in this case, because in the Polish-Lithuanian federation established in 1386 the " Ruthenian " lands (this is the only possible translation of the old name *Ruś*, which continued to be used there) enjoyed a large degree of autonomy ; released from the degrading Tartar yoke, they participated, through their representatives, in the government of a body politic which connected them more intimately than ever before with the historic European community. Since the Lithuanians also, finally converted in 1387, were now Catholics, the federation as a whole was under Catholic leadership, and new plans for reuniting the Ruthenians with Rome were considered before and after the Union of Florence. But even those of them who remained Greek Orthodox after the Union of Brest (1596) were undoubtedly included in the European community of the Renaissance, Reformation and Counter-Reformation periods, so that the eastern limits of that community certainly extended as far as the borders of the Jagellonian Federation (so called from the name of its first ruler and his dynasty), organized as a Commonwealth in 1569.[40]

But did Europe not extend even farther towards the East ? With the support of their Tartar overlords, the princes of Moscow had succeeded in uniting under their rule all of the new, colonial Russia, and in creating the Great Russian State, whose formation, chiefly in the fourteenth century, has been so competently described by A. E. Presniakov.[41] The policy of appeasement adopted by these princes in their relations with the Tartar Khans, which can be traced back to Alexander Nevsky— so courageous in his struggle against Western powers—was not completely abandoned even after a first attempt at liberation in 1380. And even the usually admitted date of the final liberation, exactly one hundred years later, is not uncontroversial, since the Golden Horde was not destroyed until 1502,[42] and not until 1547 did Moscow's ruler officially assume the title of Tsar, formerly reserved to the Tartar Khans.

It is true that before this when the Tartar power, divided into various Khanates, was obviously disintegrating, Moscow had entered into her first diplomatic relations with Europe. The treaty of 1449[43] concluded by Vasil II with his Western neighbour, Casimir of Poland and Lithuania, was only a delimitation of their respective spheres of influence, leaving each in a different orbit of culture and with a different form of government. But even before the conquest of Novgorod in 1478, and before his alliances with the Habsburgs, with Denmark, and with Hungary, Ivan III, through his " marriage at the Vatican " in 1472, raised high hopes that he would join the Western world of the Renaissance,[44] even through a religious union.

As in so many cases of similar negotiations with the Papacy, well explained in Father Pierling's basic work, not only were these expectations completely disappointed, but what happened was exactly the contrary. Instead of uniting with the real Rome, as the new Rome at the Bosphorus had tried to do before its fall, Moscow gradually elaborated the conception that she was the third and final Rome,[45] more definitely opposed to the first one than the second had been—that once admired Byzantium which, after betraying Orthodoxy through the Union of Florence, was now punished by the Turkish conquest.

Freed from her own Asiatic conquerors, Moscow nevertheless continued to develop on lines which G. Vernadsky has justly compared with the basic trends of the Ottoman Empire and—as far as the system of the first Tsar, Ivan the Terrible, is concerned—with the distinctive features of present-day Bolshevism.[46] In spite of the " anglomania " of this now admired despot, his political philosophy (which he defended in famous theoretical discussions[47]) placed his Russia outside Europe to no less an extent than it had been under the Tartars.

Strangely enough, it was another Tsar having much in

common with Ivan the Terrible, Peter the Great, who is considered—sometimes even blamed by the Slavophils—as the " Westernizer " of Russia. He is praised by excellent interpreters of modern Russia for having rejected the seventeenth-century idea of connecting his country with Europe and her culture through the intermediary of his Polish neighbours and, instead, turned directly to the most advanced Western countries.[48] And no one has gone further in stressing his success than Arnold Toynbee.[49] While Toynbee considers Russia before Peter's reforms to have been an entirely separate civilized society, distinct not only from Western, but even from Greek Orthodox culture in South-Eastern Europe, he thinks that now the continental frontier of the Western world " advanced, at one bound, from the eastern border of Poland and Sweden to the distant lines " of Russia's advance in the Eurasian steppes. Thus, he says, " the wardenship of Western society " was " suddenly snatched out of the hands " of Russia's western neighbours ; and the conclusion would be that, even if Russia herself did not immediately become the " warden " of Western society, she definitely entered that society and, as S. H. Cross puts it,[50] " caught up " with the West, in spite of the " full stop " in her development caused by the long period when the Mongol rule and its consequences had kept her outside Europe.

There are serious arguments in favour of such an interpretation, dear to all the Russian " Westerners ". The strongest European element, reacting throughout the course of Russian history against the Asiatic impact, was, of course, the Christian faith of the Russian people, which can be traced back to the mediaeval Kievan tradition,[51] and which even a certain religious dualism resulting from a survival of pre-Christian beliefs could not basically distort. The process of " Westernization ", always rather superficial in the purely Great Russian territories, was facilitated also by the inclusion of large regions which, before coming under Tsarist rule, had been associated with the West. The rôle of Kiev, which was ceded by Poland together with the left bank of the Dnieper in 1667, has been quite recently emphasized in C. Manning's *Story of the Ukraine*[52]; Peter the Great himself, who started the systematic Russification of the Ukraine, annexed the even more " Western " Baltic provinces ; and under Catherine II and Alexander I, who, to a greater extent than Peter, connected Russia with Europe, even larger purely European territories—most of Poland and what was formerly Swedish Finland—were added to the Empire. Politically that Empire was now definitely a part of the European state system, and it is obvious that from the eighteenth century European history cannot be written without including the whole foreign policy of Russia.[53] And while the earlier trends of the European mind, including the now so much better appreciated culture of the Baroque and what Paul Hazard called " the crisis of the European conscience " around 1700,[54] did not reach Russia, she was touched and influenced in an ever higher degree by intellectual movements which followed, from the Enlightenment[55] to Marxism.

But in opposition to these arguments, equally serious doubts can be expressed whether all these factors resulted in making Tsarist Russia truly European. The religious tradition was not strengthened, but suffered from reforms which started with the replacement of the Patriarch by the bureaucratic " Holy Synod ", and gradually made Russian Orthodoxy a mere auxiliary of autocracy.[56] The genuine European character of the Western acquisitions, far from penetrating into Russia proper, provoked instead a nationalistic effort, having in view their complete Russification, so that the western boundaries of Russia, one and indivisible, separating from Europe the oppressed non-Russian nationalities at that border, seem to mark the advance of an Eurasian empire under Russian control, at the expense of the historic European community. To that community, the political participation of such an overwhelmingly large extra-European empire in the European Concert constituted a permanent threat which became clearly apparent at the Congress of Vienna,[57] after the traditional balance of power had been destroyed through the partitions of Poland. Napoleon's experience, repeated one hundred years later by the Germans, now Russia's immediate neighbours, proved that it was not Russia—easy to invade, impossible to conquer—but the much smaller countries on the European continent which had to fear for their security. Finally, the various cultural trends which originated in Western Europe were all profoundly modified as soon as their ideas, and the methods of putting their ideas into practice, had been reinterpreted on Russian soil : it was there that Marxism produced Bolshevism.

It is a dangerous illusion to believe that because Hegelian dialectics, the Communist Manifesto, and the alliance between materialism and nationalism were " made in Germany ", Lenin might eventually prove to have been a " Westernizer " of Russia completing Peter's work.[58] Whatever we may think about the more or less European character of the Empire which lasted from Peter I to Nicholas II, the " Red Tsardom ", created in November 1917 after a real but vain attempt towards Westernization made in March of the same year, was and remained non-European if not anti-European. Now even the administrative boundary between the geographically European and Asiatic parts of Russia disappeared completely, the Russian Soviet Republic, by far the largest of all, extending west and east of the Urals as the nucleus of the others, and the western boundaries of the Union of Soviet Republics being, without any doubt, the eastern limit of Europe. That is the reason why the struggle for the establishment of these boundaries was much more than a territorial dispute between the Russians and their neighbours.

That struggle lasted from 1918 to 1921. It started immediately after the Armistice in World War I, since two days later the Soviets openly proclaimed their aim of including the whole of Central Europe in a Union of Communist Republics.[59] But even in the defeated countries their appeal found only a limited response, and all the non-Russian parts of Tsarist Russia had declared for complete independence as democratic, national states immediately after the November Revolution, fully aware that only thus could they join the European community of free peoples. After a hard fight against the Red invaders, all the peoples between Germany and Russia succeeded in achieving that goal, with the exception of the Ukrainians and the White Russians, who were forced to form Soviet Republics under Russian control—soon to become parts of the U.S.S.R. The Treaty of Riga (March 18, 1921), which ended the whole struggle, included some Ukrainian and White Russian minorities within the new Polish border. This frontier, like the historic frontier of the Polish Commonwealth before the Partitions, became the eastern limit of Europe, but compared with the latter it meant a withdrawal to the line of the Second Partition, in 1793.

In 1939 Soviet Russia decided to advance beyond that line, as well as north of it, in the Baltic region, and south of it, towards the Danube. The agreements between Eurasia and the equally anti-European dictatorship established in Germany, signed on August 23 and September 28, now revealed in all their secret clauses,[60] called for a partition very favourable to the Soviet Union, since all the Baltic countries, the eastern half of Poland, and formerly Rumanian Bessarabia were recognized as within its sphere of influence and thus excluded from Europe. But what proved to be even more favourable to Soviet Russia was

another partition which was the unexpected result of the
" strange alliance " between Hitler's original partner and the
Anglo-Saxon democracies. Germany and her satellites were
defeated in common, but, in addition to these satellites, all
countries east of Sweden, Germany, and Italy, including heroic
allies, with the sole exception of Greece, were forced into the
" Russian orbit "[61] and excluded from the Atlantic community.

These only too well-known facts become deeply significant,
if considered against the historic background of the whole
European Age. If they remain unchanged, the pre-war limit of
the European community on the great eastern isthmus between
the Arctic and the Black Sea, running approximately from
Petsamo to Cetatea Alba,[62] will be withdrawn to a line from
Szczecin to Trieste, on the isthmus between the Baltic and
the Adriatic. A large part of old, historic Europe would be
abandoned to Eurasia, and only a greatly reduced Europe would
join America in the coming Atlantic Age. There would be a
striking analogy with the territorial losses suffered by the
Mediterranean community at the beginning of the European
Age. But the present withdrawal would be even more painful,
both for the sacrificed peoples, which after a thousand years of
participation in the development of Europe's Christian culture
would be placed under a Communist dictatorship, and for the
new Euro-American community, which would not even gain
a frontier guaranteeing a minimum of security against new
invasions from Eurasia.

CHAPTER VI

The Geographical Divisions:
(*a*) Western and Eastern Europe

CHAPTER VI

The Geographical Divisions:
(a) Western and Eastern Europe

WEST versus East—this is the basic issue which is emphasized whenever the opposition between different regions and the corresponding spheres of culture is discussed. Such is the usual approach, recently followed in F. S. C. Northrop's provocative book,[1] of those who study the divisions of the whole globe. In this case, the East is more or less identified with Asia, and the West with Europe and her sphere of influence.

It has been pointed out in the preceding chapters that this world-wide antagonism deeply affected the course of European history : parts of geographical Europe were temporarily lost through Asiatic conquest, and European expansion over the adjacent part of Asia resulted in the formation of an Eurasian sub-continent. But a similar problem of relations between West and East exists also within the limits of the historic European community. This became particularly evident when, at the end of our study of these limits, we tried to discover the eastern frontier of European history. Therefore, as we now turn to the divisions of that history, it seems advisable to start this time, not with the chronological, but with the geographical aspects, and first to consider the following questions: *Is* there a basic difference between the western and the eastern part of historic Europe, and if so, *where* is the internal dividing line, parallel to the Atlantic limit of Europe in the west and to the Asiatic limit in the east ?

These vital questions have never been studied more thoroughly than in the address which the Czech historian Jaroslav Bidlo made in 1933 before the International Congress of Historical Sciences in Warsaw,[2] and in the discussion which he provoked.[3] Answering the first question, Bidlo made it quite clear that in his opinion the current distinction between Western and Eastern Europe is fully justified by a basic dualism of European history. For him, the differences between these two parts of Europe were not merely a result of their geographical position, but very real and essential. Tracing them back to the opposition between Rome and Byzantium, particularly in the religious sphere, he answered the second question, concerning the limit between Western and Eastern Europe, by identifying the latter with the area controlled by the Greek Orthodox Church.

Bidlo did not raise the question as to which parts of the various Russias and which periods of their past belong to European history. He included them all but considered them, of course, together with Byzantium, typically Eastern European. And following his religious criterion, he also included in Eastern Europe all the other Orthodox peoples, most of them Slavonic like the Russians. The remaining parts of Europe, outside the realm of the Orthodox Church, would constitute Western Europe.

But even for those who fully agree with Bidlo as to the decisive importance of the religious factor in all history and the special significance of all problems of Christianity in European history, it is difficult to accept his interpretation. From the point of view of religious doctrine and even of ecclesiastical organization, the differences between Protestantism and both Catholicism and Orthodoxy are much greater than those which separate the two latter. And yet nobody would question that Protestant as well as Catholic nations belong to the same Western Europe. Furthermore, religious differences, important as they are, especially when they are differences between Christians and non-Christians, must not be considered the sole basis for tracing the historic divisions within the Christian community of Europe. As a matter of fact, such an interpretation leads in practice to rather doubtful conclusions.

A first danger is evidenced in Toynbee's and de Reynold's conceptions, which, without being influenced by Bidlo, come very near to his conclusion. The English scholar, a specialist in Greek history of all ages, is fully aware of the profound differences between South-Eastern Europe and Russia, in spite of their common Orthodox faith. But he opposes both of these Orthodox societies to Western Christian society,[4] so that the idea of European unity vanishes altogether. And G. de Reynold goes to the extreme logical consequence of such an approach, saying that there are two Europes, Western and Eastern, of which only the former is really European.[5]

Such an impression is understandable if Russia, without any territorial or chronological distinctions, is included in Eastern Europe in spite of the non-European features of her history, and if, in view of her tremendous expansion, she is considered the very core of such an Eastern Europe, at least from the fall of the Byzantine Empire. But that leads immediately to another danger. The same Bidlo who so strongly stresses the unity of all Orthodox peoples in contradistinction to Western Christendom, tried to show in another much larger work[6] the unity of all Slavic history, including, of course, the Catholic Slavs. That would justify the exclusion of even these Western Slavs from Western Europe, the only real Europe, and naturally a few other peoples, neither Orthodox nor even Slavic but inseparable from them geographically and historically—the Hungarians and the Baltic nations—would suffer a similar treatment.

Reacting against such a misinterpretation, which became particularly shocking when the Soviet system clearly placed Russia outside any Europe, while the liberated nations between Russia and Germany turned more than ever before towards the West, some scholars limited the conception of Eastern Europe to these very nations. For the French historian Michel Lhéritier,[7] that " Europe orientale ", eastern in the geographical sense, was politically and culturally very definitely part of Europe as a whole and closely connected with the Latin West, since even its Orthodox members had little, if anything, in common with Soviet Russia. Moreover, quite recently even Hugh Seton Watson,[8] writing with much sympathy towards Soviet Russia and her growing influence, called " Eastern Europe " only the group of countries west of the U.S.S.R., whether Catholic or Orthodox.

Such an Eastern Europe, with its truly European variety of comparatively small countries, has, indeed, much more in common with Western Europe than with the colossal neighbour in the East, the Eurasian Empire, which, under the appearances of Soviet federalism, is even more uniform " in content " than it was under the Tsars.[9] As far as that huge intermediary area between Europe proper and Asia proper is concerned, our examination of Europe's eastern boundary has shown that even its geographically European section was never fully integrated in the historic European community. Furthermore, discussing the position of Russia, whose name is so frequently used in a general sense which would cover all the Eastern Slavs, we had to distinguish between Russia proper, or Great Russia, on the one hand and old Ruś, or Ruthenia—including the Ukraine (sometimes called Little Russia), as well as White Russia—on the other hand ; between the Russia of Novgorod and the Russia of Moscow ; and, finally, between various periods of Russian history : not only before and after Peter the Great, but also before and after the Mongol invasion, and before and after the Bolshevik Revolution. And taking into consideration the problem of Orthodoxy, one more distinction must be added, which is a twofold one : first, between Russia, in the largest sense, before and after the Eastern schism ; and, secondly, between those regions which on various occasions accepted a religious reunion with Rome and those which always rejected that idea.[10]

Some of these distinctions are at the same time a serious warning against the oversimplified conception of permanent boundaries between cultural regions, drawn once for all. Just as the chronological divisions of history cannot be based upon individual dates, but must be made in consideration of shorter or longer transition periods, so the territorial divisions must not fail to take into account the existence of smaller and larger zones of transition, where the cultural frontiers are shifting back and forth. This is a typical feature of historical geography, which must reckon with the factor of human evolution, and it is important to remember it in order to reach clear definitions, not only of Europe as a whole, but also of its various regions.

As far as Eastern Europe, which cannot be simply identified with Orthodox Europe, is concerned, all that has been said suggests a preliminary definition, both negative and positive.

Eastern European history is *not* the history of Russia plus that of a few smaller countries, mostly Orthodox and Slavonic, in Russia's sphere of influence. That misconception, which can be partly explained by the transitory situation of the nineteenth century in which the study of Eastern European history was started in a Germany allied with Russia, is now threatening to arise again out of the situation which followed the last war. What is involved is not only a wrong delimitation of Eastern Europe, placing it beyond the limits of " real " Europe, but also a completely inadequate treatment of all non-Russian parts of that whole region, reducing their histories to mere appendices of Russian history.

On the contrary, Eastern Europe must be considered an integral part of " real " Europe, and its history consists of two equally important sections. One of them is indeed the history of those Eastern Slavs and of those periods of their past which are definitely European ; in the study of this section, the non-European, Asiatic impact must be carefully considered and clearly distinguished as a foreign element. But Eastern European history also includes the stories of a large group of nations between the various Russias and Western Europe, and it is precisely that second—or rather, first—section of Eastern Europe which was, and still is, the frequently ignored stepchild of European history and historiography. In order to understand its real position, it might be advisable to give first a definition of Western Europe itself. The *terra ignota* east of it will then appear more clearly in its extension and significance.

What is Western Europe ? The question seems easy, since no other term is more frequently used in the writing of history, as well as in current political discussions. But it is mostly used in such a vague sense that its unequivocal simplicity is rather fallacious. The name Western Europe suffers, first of all, from its purely relative character, which it has in common with so many other misleading terms. For that very reason some doubts have been expressed above whether it is advisable to call our civilization " Western ". But when we speak of Western Europe, we do not always think of a cultural, but sometimes merely of a geographical, region, and that, of course, increases the danger of confusion.

One thing at least has appeared with growing clarity in the present discussion : Western Europe cannot be identified with Europe proper ; since then the addition of the word " Western " would be completely useless. And it is equally evident that

Western Europe, as an historic concept, was formed of two
different parts, easy to distinguish if we remember the transition
from the Mediterranean to the European Age and the earliest
territorial division of our continent, into an " old " and " new"
Europe.

Western Europe includes, of course, in the first place and as
its cradle, the European part of the western, Roman section of
the Mediterranean world, and the non-Mediterranean territories
which were added through Roman conquest. That means Italy,
the Iberian peninsula, Gaul, most of Britain, and the Roman-
controlled parts of Germany up to the *limes* connecting the
Rhine and the Danube. In the earliest divisions of the Empire,
Illyricum was attached to the Western part, but that region
east of the Adriatic Sea became an object of endless controversies, both political and ecclesiastical, with the Eastern
Empire.[11] The influence of the East proved stronger, for obvious
geographical reasons which, after the Slavic penetration into
the disputed territory, were strengthened by ethnic factors.

During the " making of Europe " the western part of " old "
Europe was considerably enlarged. It remains, however, to
determine which parts of " new " Europe, outside the limits
of the Roman Empire, became associated with its western half.
No doubt is possible with regard to the rest of Britain, Ireland,
and the other islands in the north-western direction. Entering
the European community, they became, of course, part of
Western Europe, which here extended simply to the extreme
limits of geographical Europe, as explained in an earlier
chapter.[12] But what about the extension beyond the Rhine-
Danube line ? Did these additions in the north-eastern
direction, into the very heart of " new " Europe, also become
parts of the enlarged Western Europe ?

If only two parts of Europe are distinguished, so that the alter-
native is simply West or East, then this important question will

not be too difficult to answer. One thing, however, must be well understood in advance : a positive answer will not necessarily mean that the Western Europe so enlarged remained entirely homogeneous. On the contrary, a further study of the regional divisions of Europe will reveal the development of very different regions within the western half of the continent.

Returning, with such a reservation in mind, to the issue now under discussion, it must be stressed that the north-eastern extension of Western Europe was achieved in connection with the two successive restorations of the Western Empire : in 800 and 962. That the Empire of Charlemagne was completely Western is beyond any possible doubt. It is true that to the original area of the Frankish Kingdom, formed on formerly Roman territory, were added not only other parts of that territory in Gaul and Italy, but also, in the East, sections of Germany which never had been under the Romans. Similarly, beyond the boundaries of the Empire proper, Marches were created, not only in Northern Spain, but more particularly along the whole eastern border, in ethnically non-German, predominantly Slavic territories.[13] As long, however, as these outposts were only supposed to protect the main body of the Empire, its basic character as a union of Gaul, Germany and most of Italy was not really altered.

Nevertheless, in the divisions of Charlemagne's heritage there already appeared very distinctly the problem of West versus East, thanks to the creation of a West Frankish and an East Frankish kingdom. Without touching here the question of the division between the two, either through an intermediary territory, the *regnum Lotharii*, or through an always controversial frontier line, it is obvious that the eastern kingdom, which became the Germany of the future, had in the east its greatest possibilities for a comparatively easy expansion. And after the second restoration of the Western Empire, which was a *translatio* of the imperial power to the kings of Germany, that eastern expansion continued with even more vigour.

In all discussions about the so-called Holy Roman Empire,[14] the question is raised whether an imperial policy primarily concerned with Italy did not frequently divert the attention of Germany's rulers from that more vital, more specifically German problem of *Ostpolitik*.[15] That may be so, but hardly less important is another question : whether the imperial authority of their kings, the practical identification of Germany with the Empire, did not greatly facilitate for the Germans eastern conquests far beyond the most ambitious plans of the Roman Emperors of antiquity. These plans had included the domination of all Germany, and it has been rightly pointed out[16] that their failure—the fact that Germany never was completely under the Romans—had far-reaching consequences both for the old Roman Empire and the future of Europe. Nevertheless, when the German Kingdom of the tenth century became not only a part of the restored Western Empire but its very nucleus, the belated inclusion of Germany as a whole in Western Europe seemed to be an accomplished fact. But was imperial Germany in a position to make additional, non-German territories also truly " Western " ?

Strangely enough, the whole region north of Germany, *i.e.*, Scandinavia, which never was supposed to be included in the Empire (attempts in that direction having failed even in the case of Denmark),[17] became undoubtedly part of Western Europe as soon as it was converted to the Christian faith. That extension of Western Christendom which soon, through Swedish conquest, included Finland also, proved a lasting success achieved without German interference. On the contrary, all the efforts of Germany's military might and diplomacy, all German pretensions to the rôle of *Kulturträger* for Western Europe, proved insufficient to achieve the aim of

Germany's eastern policy. Since the unification of both Empires, Western and Eastern, proved to be an illusion even at the height of the power of the Ottonians or the Hohenstaufen,[18] that aim was the inclusion in the Western Empire, the Holy Roman Empire of the German Nation, of all lands which were not under the Eastern, Byzantine Empire.

That policy met, however, with the resistance of these non-German peoples. While ready, and in most cases even anxious, to accept, with the Christian faith, the culture of Western Europe, they were equally anxious to remain outside and independent of any Empire, either Western or Eastern, as they had always been. The German advance,[19] proceeding by degrees, with the creation of new Marches as the first step, using also the subtle methods of feudal relationship, resumed time and again after temporary withdrawals, did not succeed in establishing any clear and definite frontier line of Western Europe. That frontier seemed final only in those cases where the extermination or Germanization of the native population made political and ethnic boundaries identical. Those Slavic tribes which rejected Christianity together with German domination paid heavily for their tragic mistake. Today, however, transfers of populations may change again a situation which was the most lasting result of the famous *Drang nach Osten*.

In one case only did the Germans succeed in forcing their suzerainty over a Christian state which non-Germans had created east of them, and in making that Slavic state, gradually elevated to the rank of a kingdom, an integral part of the Holy Roman Empire. The kingdom of Bohemia, frequently called the Empire's " noblest " member, occupied, however, such an exceptional position[20] that it is the most typical example of an intermediary region between Western and Eastern Europe.

Entirely different are the cases of Poland and Hungary, the two Catholic kingdoms of Eastern Europe, to the latter of which the Catholic kingdom of Croatia was united from the end of the eleventh century.[21] Both had been from their formation, one hundred years before, Eastern outposts of Western culture, which they tried to acquire from non-German, Latin sources.[22] But at the same time, steadily rejecting imperial overlordship, they were the defences against Western —i.e., German—conquest of an Eastern Europe which, after all that has been said about Western Europe, is now much easier to define.

There is an evident analogy in the formation and constitution of both Western and Eastern Europe. In both cases a clear distinction must be made between the original territory and the areas which were added later. In the case of Eastern Europe that difference is so striking that North-Eastern and South-Eastern Europe are frequently opposed to each other in the practice of historiography.[23]

But the analogy goes even further. Just as the original part of Western Europe is identical with the Roman section of old, Mediterranean Europe, including its conquests at the threshold of the European Age, so South-Eastern Europe is nothing but the European part of the eastern section of the Empire—the Greek part of old Mediterranean Europe, plus its extension under the Romans to the lower Danube.

This first point is plain and uncontroversial. The difficulties of interpretation begin as soon as the problem of North-Eastern Europe is considered. It is, of course, impossible to speak, as in the case of Western Europe, of the expansion of a restored Empire, transferred to a new nation. The Eastern Empire lasted without interruption until the Ottoman invasion, and before 1453 never had to be " restored " in another form. Constantinople was never conquered by Slavic nations, in spite of the imperial ambitions of Bulgarian and Serbian leaders, and it was only briefly, and in a late period, held by the Latins. From the sixth century, when Greek took the place of Latin as the official language,[24] until the final catastrophe, the uninterrupted line of the βασιλεῖς τῶν Ῥωμαίων, notwithstanding the ethnic origin of their successive dynasties, perpetuated the Empire of Constantinople in its Greek form.

That Empire, even in the times of its greatest power, was hardly able to defend, either in Europe or in Asia, its ancient Roman boundaries. The outermost north-eastern conquest of Roman days, the only conquest beyond the Danube—Dacia—was lost before the Empire was divided. That area, whatever we may think of the question of Rumanian continuity, always remained an area of transition between South-Eastern and North-Eastern Europe, even after the Ottoman Sultans had replaced the Greek Emperors. The latter, who never attempted to reconquer old Dacia, were even less well equipped—nor were they anxious—to conquer any integral part of North-Eastern Europe. Even the most powerful Macedonian dynasty failed to secure to the Empire either its former possessions in Pannonia or its ancient foothold at the northern shores of the Black Sea. The temporary reconquest of what the Bulgarians had occupied in the Balkan peninsula remained the greatest military and political success.[25]

There was, indeed, under that same Macedonian dynasty a tremendous cultural expansion of Byzantium in the north-eastern direction, through the medium of the Greek Orthodox Church, initiated even before the first Macedonian Emperor by the great Patriarch Photius. It seems, therefore, well justified to say that precisely this sphere of cultural influence must be added to old South-Eastern Europe in order to arrive at a correct conception of Eastern Europe as a whole. But two questions immediately arise in that connection.

It must be asked, first, whether it has to be admitted in advance that all the territories, even the most distant, where the Greek Orthodox faith was introduced became through that mere fact a permanent and integral part of Eastern Europe. Toynbee realizes the profound difference between far-away Russia and the original home of Greek Orthodox society, and therefore declares that " offshoot " to be a distinct society in itself.[26] Differing in that respect from Bidlo's theory, he is obviously right as far as Muscovite Russia is concerned. But without repeating what has been said above about the eastern limits of Europe as a whole and about the various Russias, let us simply note that Orthodoxy alone offers no conclusive evidence that a given country is part of Eastern Europe. And that leads to the second question : whether only Orthodox countries should be included in the conception of Eastern Europe.

Before answering this, it must be recalled that in the days of Byzantium's great cultural expansion the Eastern Church was not yet definitely separated from the Western. It was always well known that the Photian schism was by no means final. Today F. Dvorník is trying to show that it was not a real schism at all.[27] He has proved, at least, that Saints Cyrill and Methodius, those Greek " apostles of the Slavs ", could be, at the same time, loyal to Photius and to Rome. He has also shown that their activity, including their defence of the Eastern rite, left lasting traces in countries which always remained Catholic.[28] Moreover, even those countries which gradually were affected by the Cerularian schism of 1054—this time a real break between Rome and Byzantium which was to be final— always remained interested, together with Byzantium itself and in contradistinction to Muscovite Russia alone, in projects and possibilities of reunion. The history of religious union between the Eastern and the Western Churches is, indeed, inseparable from the history of their division.[29] And therefore that division is no sufficient ground for a basic division of Europe.

It is true that the religious difference between Catholics, even those—or, rather, particularly those—of Eastern rite, and the Orthodox greatly embittered political controversies between Slavs, even such as are so close to each other as, for instance, Croats and Serbs. But on the other hand there also was, as early as in the Middle Ages, a Slavic solidarity, either cultural, through the community of the *nobile linguagium Slavonicum*,[30] or political, in reaction to a common danger from the Germans and their Empire. And it was precisely the Catholic Slavs who first and most directly were exposed to that danger.

Likewise threatened were the non-Slavic peoples sooner or later converted to the Catholic faith—the Hungarians, Lithuanians, Latvians, and Estonians—peoples whose history, like the history of the Orthodox Rumanians, is practically inseparable from Slavic history. All these nations east of Germany, nations which in spite of their Catholicism and Western culture never receive sufficient attention in any separate treatment of Western European history, constitute together with their Orthodox neighbours, as far as these remained in the European community, the new, northern part of Eastern Europe, which in the European Age appeared beside old South-Eastern Europe.

Eastern Europe would, therefore, be the region between the Holy Roman Empire, or the Teutonic and Romance nations, on the one hand, and Eurasian Russia, i.e., those Eastern Slavs who found themselves in certain periods of history outside the European community, on the other hand. In other words, it is that large and important part of Europe of which the Byzantine Empire only—all too frequently studied in isolation—is duly considered in general historiography, at least since the rebirth of Byzantine studies some fifty years ago ; all the other countries of that region are usually treated on the margin either of Western European history, if they are Catholic, or of Russian history, if they are Orthodox or Slavic or both.

It is true that this region as a whole never had any political unity ; no Empire could expect to control it all. But neither was Western Europe ever completely unified politically, in spite of the many attempts and claims of the Empire restored by the Germans. It is also true that there was in Eastern Europe a far greater lack of cultural unity than in Western Europe, but the basic elements of unity, common to the whole of Europe, especially the great traditions of Antiquity and Christianity, were equally strong in both parts, and the element of internal variety, more striking in the Eastern, is in itself typically European. It merely makes the historian distinguish, within the frontiers of Eastern Europe, smaller regions which correspond to the various trends of political and cultural development.

It is hardly necessary to point out that, like the external frontier separating Eastern Europe from Western Eurasia, these internal divisions are not fixed by any permanent lines, but fluctuate in areas of transition. In that respect it proved decisive that the Danubian frontier between old, imperial South-Eastern Europe and the new territories of the North-East was gradually replaced by a Danubian region, smaller but almost as important as the other two regions and sometimes an object of controversy between them. There appear, therefore, in Eastern Europe not two, but three main divisions, and each of them passed through at least three phases of development which correspond more or less, as we shall see later, to the chronological divisions of European history.

The first of these territorial sections of Eastern Europe remains, of course, the South-East, the Eastern, Byzantine Empire, together with the states created by the Slavs in the Balkan peninsula. Together with them, the Greek Empire was conquered by the Turks, and under their Asiatic Empire that original section, in the second phase of its evolution, ceased to be really part of Europe, as we have pointed out in a previous chapter.[31] The division of the Balkans among the Christian successor states of the Ottoman Empire reunited that region with Europe during the last period of its history.

Temporarily the Turks penetrated far into the Danubian region, conquering the centre of Hungary and extending their suzerainty over Transylvania, Wallachia and Moldavia. Before that invasion most of this region was controlled by the Hungarian kingdom, surrounded by vassal lands and temporarily united, through dynastic ties, with Poland, in the third region of Eastern Europe, and with Bohemia, in the intermediary zone between Eastern and Western Europe. After the period of Ottoman penetration the Austrian Habsburgs, who had long ago claimed the Hungarian succession, united the whole Danubian region, except what was to be Rumania, in an Empire of changing constitution, but always, in one way or another, connected with Germany. That situation, which will be discussed in the following chapter, lasted until the recent division of the Habsburg monarchy into another group of successor states.

North-Eastern Europe, the third region if the Danubian is treated separately, consisted originally of Poland and old Kievan Russia—preferably called Ruś or Ruthenia. In the following period both were federated, together with the younger Grand-Duchy of Lithuania, under the Jagellonian dynasty, the same which for a short time ruled also over the Danubian region. The partition of the Polish Commonwealth between the Russian and German Empires made that third region disappear completely for more than a hundred years, creating the impression that there was nothing between Western

European Germany and a new Russia, identified with Eastern Europe. The crucial significance of that "heartland" of Europe[32] reappeared, however, as soon as it was liberated, and will also be studied in the next chapter.

What has been said here will suffice to indicate the complex and sometimes decisive rôle of a badly neglected Eastern Europe, inseparable from Western Europe, in the whole course of European history. In conclusion, it might be added that while Western Europe is predominantly, though not exclusively —for the Celts cannot be forgotten—Romance and Germanic, Eastern Europe is predominantly, though even less exclusively, Slavonic. But since the Slavs are divided into Catholic and Orthodox, since so many other peoples, from the Greeks in the south to the Balts and Finns in the north, are associated with them, and since the colonization process of the Eastern Slavs has placed many of them outside Europe, another contrast ought to be stressed. Western Europe was formed around the restored Western Empire, while Eastern Europe included what remained of the Eastern Empire plus the part of the continent which succeeded in remaining outside any Empire.

Another conclusion is even more important. Eastern Europe, as defined here, is no less European than Western Europe. As soon as the identification of Eastern Europe with the realm of Orthodoxy or—what is much more misleading—with Russia is abandoned, it appears that the eastern part of Europe, far from being uniform, is even richer in variety than the western. Precisely because Eastern Europe is not a cultural unit, it participates in both the Greek and the Roman form of Europe's Ancient and Christian heritage. In Eastern Europe it has been tried time and again, though unfortunately without complete and lasting success, to reconcile these two expressions of the European mind. And it was Eastern Europe—not as a whole, since it never was organized as a political unit, but through its individual nations or regional federations—which defended the whole of Europe, its faith and its culture, against the repeated onslaughts of the Asiatic powers that crossed the Straits in the south or advanced on the wide isthmus north of the Black Sea.

CHAPTER VII

The Geographical Divisions:
(b) The Dualism of Central Europe

CHAPTER VII

The Geographical Divisions:
(b) The Dualism of Central Europe

THERE is something arbitrary in all divisions of history, in the geographical perhaps even more than in the chronological. In the case of European history, the shortcomings of any such division are particularly evident—one might even say un-avoidable—if it is admitted in advance that it must be a division into two parts only. That is precisely the reason why so frequently a third part of Europe is distinguished in addition to, or rather between, the two basic parts in the West and in the East. And it is only natural, and in agreement with the relative character of the whole terminology which is being used almost traditionally, that this additional section of the continent is called Central Europe. There is, however, no agreement as to the meaning of that name, and at least two different interpretations must be distinguished, each of them typical of the peace-planning and of the " propaganda " during one of the two World Wars. These interpretations have so deeply influenced, and continue to influence, not only political science, but also historiography, that they deserve careful consideration.

During the European War of 1914–1918, no political treatise was more discussed than Friedrich Naumann's *Mitteleuropa*,[1] published in 1915, when the military situation seemed favour-able to the so-called " central " powers, and their leaders wanted to define and to popularize their war aims. During the World War of 1939–1945, the plans of the Third *Reich*, much more ambitious than those of the Second had been, reached far beyond Naumann's conception of Central Europe, being influenced instead by Haushofer's only too well-known " geopolitical " analysis of the whole world.[2] From the point of view of European history and its divisions, the peace-planning of the anti-German coalition was, therefore, more instructive. And this time it was among the Allies, particularly those east of Germany, that the problem of Central Europe was most thoroughly studied. The bibliography of all that was published on that problem is simply amazing,[3] but it must be noted at once that the amount of material which had to be examined resulted, at least in part, from the significant fact that this time Central Europe was considered in close connection with Eastern Europe.

As far as the terminology is concerned, it became even more confusing than before. A new expression even appeared—Central-Eastern Europe—which, although it was used by official organizations,[4] was never sufficiently clarified ; at the same time, the old *Mitteleuropa* idea, while not disappearing entirely, entered its " final stage ". Felix Gilbert, who recently stressed this point,[5] tried to simplify the issue for American readers by suggesting that both the terms *Mitteleuropa* and Central Europe should be used, the former to be associated with the old German conception and the latter with the ideas advanced during the last war.

This seems a doubtful solution, however, because, after all, the expressions are completely equivalent, only taken from two different languages. It ought to be admitted instead that there is within the limits of any possible central section of Europe, from whatever language its name should be taken, a basic dualism, perhaps more striking than the dualism which some scholars have wanted to see in the historic structure of Europe as a whole.

There appears, first of all, to be a profound dualism, or even discrepancy, of political programmes. In the German interpretation the whole of Central Europe would be united, one way or another, under German leadership, and for that reason the German name of that section of Europe may seem suggestive. According to Germany's opponents, the eastern part of Central Europe, which is quite different from the western, ought to be independent of Germany, and possibly united in one or more federations or confederations which would be the best guarantee of independence and security.

But even in the German conception it is evident that, independently of any political solution of the problem, there is in Central Europe a dualism which clearly distinguishes from one another its western and its eastern parts. The western is really German, ethnically and historically : it simply is identical with Germany proper. The eastern part, which can be called East-Central Europe, but not Central-Eastern Europe (this would mean the central part of Eastern Europe, hence something entirely different), might come under German control, as it actually did, totally or in part, in various periods of history; nevertheless, that area which the Germans consider their closest sphere of influence in the east always remained non-German, inhabited by a great variety of ethnic and linguistic groups in contradistinction to the homogeneously German West-Central Europe. Only a complete extermination, expulsion or thorough Germanization of these groups could have changed the situation. But none of these methods, though all were tried at given moments, has proved fully successful in the course of history. The success remained limited to local shifts of the frontier between West-Central Europe and East-Central Europe, to the advantage of the western, German part.

That very issue has already been discussed above, in connection with the problem of the shifting frontier between

Western and Eastern Europe. And this is only natural. For if Europe is divided, with a view to a better understanding of European history, into three parts instead of only two, then both Western and Eastern Europe—the two primary, most conventional divisions—must be reduced in area in order to obtain a Central Europe formed at the expense of both of them. The question merely is whether such an interpretation is justified and gives us a geographical division of Europe less arbitrary and with fewer shortcomings than the other one.

A strong argument in favour of such an approach is the obvious fact that any analysis of either Western or Eastern Europe discovers various regions within the limits of both of them. If the two main divisions of Europe were completely homogeneous, the creation of a third one would be artificial nonsense. The preceding chapter has shown that this is not so. In Western Europe, there are territories which not only geographically—this would be a truism with little meaning— but historically are less " Western " than the others, and similarly, some parts of Eastern Europe appear less " Eastern " than the rest. In both cases this is a natural consequence of the gradual growth and expansion of each of the two regions, and of their formation out of " old " and " new " sections. In the case of Eastern Europe it also is a consequence of processes of colonization which extended Europe as a whole. On the other hand, the eastern part of Western Europe and the western part of Eastern Europe, close neighbours as they are, were necessarily in constant relations with one another, influenced each other, and had many problems in common.

But should they, therefore, be considered a unit distinct from the two other parts of Europe ? According to the German interpretation, they *are* such a unit, were it only as a result of German expansion and colonization in the eastern direction, which made the eastern, non-German part of Central Europe a German *Kulturboden*.[6] German archaeologists would add that these territories had all been originally Teutonic,[7] while German political science and demography would claim them as German *Lebensraum*. Even before Nazism popularized that conception and extended it almost indefinitely, Pan-Germanism in its earlier phase[8] had always aimed at the inclusion of all the borderlands between the compact ethnical territories of Germany proper and Russia proper, where German minorities were scattered almost everywhere among so many different smaller ethnic groups.

Such a political programme of clearly imperialistic character is, however, in spite of its old, mediaeval tradition, no sufficient reason for the scholar to accept a geographical division of Europe based upon such onesided considerations. Such a division would be at least as arbitrary as the usual distinction of Western and Eastern Europe. It would involve even more shortcomings, since it could be used, and as a matter of fact has already been used, as an argument in favour of political solutions forced upon the larger half of the Central European peoples. These non-German Central Europeans, fearing the domination of the whole of Central Europe by the strongest nation of that region, always emphasized that *their* Central Europe, the eastern part, without claiming in turn any supremacy over the western, had the right to a separate, independent existence. The long series of German acts of aggression before and during the last war made these peoples particularly aware of the danger which they all had to face, and suggested the contemporary plans for an organization of a Central Europe without Germany. And that conception, far from being a new invention, is in full agreement with Central Europe's basic dualism.

This being so, it seems obvious that what connects the histories of the two parts of Central Europe is not any real community, but rather an agelong struggle[9] against a unification enforced by the smaller, but more homogeneous and therefore stronger, part. It would be entirely artificial to pretend that these two parts have more in common with each other than the western part has with Western Europe or the eastern part with Eastern Europe. The question even arises whether there would not be greater justification for stressing the ties, political or cultural or both, which in so many periods of history connected Western Europe proper with the eastern part of Central Europe,[10] and its western part with Eastern Europe proper. Such an approach seems contrary to the most obvious geographical facts and therefore almost paradoxical, especially for those who are influenced by geographical determinism. But the very possibility of asking that surprising question makes the historian wonder whether the most adequate geographical division of Europe would not be a division, into neither two nor three, but into four parts.

A review of these four regions ought to proceed from the West towards the East. The first of them would be, of course, a Western Europe fully deserving that name, Western Europe proper. Territorially it would be almost identical with the ancient, original part of Western Europe : the European section of the ancient, truly Roman, Empire plus the small area of the British isles unconquered by the Romans and minus the small area of Germany really controlled by the Romans. Ethnically it would be the domain of the Romance and Celtic nations, including only those Germanic elements which were completely absorbed and assimilated by the Latin world and those which contributed to the formation of the Anglo-Saxon world, far away from their Central European homeland.

Included in that Western Europe proper must also be those small nations along the controversial, fluctuating, western border of Germany, which were constituted through the separation of their respective territories from the German Empire. That process started in the later Middle Ages with the formation of the Swiss Confederation[11] and of the Burgundian State ;[12] it was accelerated by the Treaty of Westphalia, which recognized the full independence of both Switzerland and the United Provinces of the Netherlands, but it was not completed before the nineteenth century, when Belgium and Luxemburg finally achieved that same objective. It was a typically European process, showing the constructive rôle of small nations, and in some cases also of federal government ; a contribution to the peaceful settlement of involved and protracted territorial disputes ; and finally a test of how the German mind can be transformed when freed from any imperialistic power complex and offered an opportunity of close co-operation with Latin elements, racial and cultural, in limited political units with specific national characters.

Through that process the two transition zones in the Low Countries and in the Alps were definitely associated with the original part of Western Europe, increasing the variety of its structure. Never was that association more evident than in the present transition from the European to the Atlantic Age, and no part of Europe is more indisputably Atlantic, although neither Luxemburg nor Switzerland have access to the sea. The temptation of limiting the new Atlantic community to that first part of Europe only, although it must be rejected for reasons given above and others which will be added later, can be easily explained by the fact that turning eastward, to the next of the four constituent parts of the European continent, we immediately enter a completely different region : Germany.

It would be absurd to include that country in any kind of Eastern Europe. Therefore, as explained in the preceding chapter, if there are only two alternatives, Germany must be considered part of Western Europe. But this is precisely one of the doubtful features of such an oversimplified division. It makes us overlook the fact that the Empire which was restored —or rather created—at the very beginning of the European Age, in 962, and, in spite of two successive renovations, in 1871 and 1933, fell at its very end, was, within the European community, a world in itself. With the Roman Empire it had little more in common than a name, which was gradually replaced by the name German, a name first added to the other,[13] then adopted in current use, and finally made official. The continuity between ancient Rome and the mediaeval Empire was a mere fiction, except at the very beginning, in the minds of an Otto III and his collaborators,[14] while there *is* a continuity between the three Empires which in German are all called *Reich*. Also fiction was the identification of the first of these three German Empires with Christendom and with the European community, a fiction opposed even in the Middle Ages by practically all non-Germans[15] and even by most of the Italians, who were, in part, forced to recognize the authority of the German king and to see him crowned in Rome. That opposition was almost as strong as the resistance against the German conquest of Europe in the recent days of the second and third *Reich*.

It is true that there appeared, even after Otto III and outside Germany, noble minds whose interpretation of mediaeval universalism not only accepted but glorified the idea of imperial leadership. If, however, Dante's unsurpassed vision of a peacefully united Christendom[16] had been the work of a Guelf instead of a Ghibellin, the synthesis of the political philosophy of the Middle Ages would have been entirely different. So it became an almost traditional attitude of Catholic historiography to idealize the power which had been the most persistent and dangerous opponent of the Papacy. And until recently, thanks to Lord Bryce's classic work,[17]

Protestant Anglo-Saxon historians also have looked with almost nostalgic admiration upon the Holy Roman Empire which Toynbee has dared to call merely the ghost of a defunct " universal state ", harmful to the great conception of the Christian Republic.[18]

German historians are at pains to show[19] that the Emperors themselves did not claim any real domination beyond the frontiers of Germany, but only some kind of overlordship, which, after all, was in the interest of European unity and therefore acceptable to the non-German nations. But even such a claim as this, coming from the kings of any individual nation, would necessarily produce in that nation a tradition of imperialism ; in the given case, it found its modern expression in the political programme of Pan-Germanism. And strangely enough, in spite of its racial inspiration, that programme aimed first at the control, not so much of all Germanic peoples, including the geographically isolated Scandinavian group, as of that Central European region where German expansion was making so much progress at the expense of the eastern neighbours.

When, therefore, German nationalism, after the disappearance of the first *Reich*, demanded the unification of Germany on national grounds, it wanted to include not only the non-German parts of the Holy Roman Empire—a claim which was rejected, on behalf of the Czechs, in Palacky's famous letter of 1848[20]—but also, to a certain extent, those non-German parts of the two strongest German states, Prussia and Austria, which always had remained outside the borders of the old Empire and the German Confederation of 1815. In the case of Prussia, her Polish provinces were, indeed, incorporated in the Second *Reich*.[21] The case of Austria was much more involved and certainly constitutes the most difficult issue in the whole Central European problem.

On the one hand, the Habsburg Empire, constituted in 1804,

two years before the Holy Roman Empire was dissolved, had in many respects better reasons for being considered the rightful heir of the latter than had the Hohenzollern Empire of 1871.[22] But, on the other hand, it included such large and diverse non-German territories that any plan, like that of Prince Felix v. Schwarzenberg, in 1849–50,[23] to make the whole of it a part—even the leading part—of a Greater Germany frightened not only all non-German powers and peoples, but even the exponents of German nationalism, which might have been submerged by foreign elements within such a " monster Empire ".

Bismarck himself preferred to see the Austrian Germans excluded, as they were in 1866, from German unity,[24] but left in control of a second Central European Empire, soon to be closely allied (from 1879 to its fall in 1918) with the other one, which alone was called German. But it was precisely that disguised form of German control over the whole of *Mitteleuropa*, contrary to the principles of the 1867 Constitution of the Habsburg Monarchy and to the real interests and aspirations of most of its peoples, which was the main cause of Austria-Hungary's disintegration.[25]

Among all the so-called successor-states, only the new, almost purely German, Republic of Austria seemed to belong, as in the past, to the western German part of Central Europe. Yet the *Anschluss*, which, as evidenced in 1938, could easily lead to a complete annihilation of Austria's historic individuality, was not the only solution of the problem created by the St. Germain Treaty.[26] The new Austria, an Alpine state with a federal constitution, might also develop into another Switzerland : not merely a state, but a real nation,[27] distinct from Germany in spite of a common racial and cultural background, as happened in the case of the Germans of Switzerland, Luxemburg, or the Low Countries. Such an Austria could form, together with Switzerland, a geographical link between Western Europe, in the proper sense, and the Eastern part of Central Europe, a similar link being constituted in the north by the Scandinavian countries.

As to the other successor-states of the Habsburg monarchy, it is obvious that they all belong to the eastern, non-German part of Central Europe, in spite of the German influence which penetrated them under Habsburg rule.[28] But they are not the only members of East-Central Europe. That name was and frequently is given, in contemporary political discussions, to the whole dozen countries, in addition to Austria, which, between the last two wars, existed as independent states between Scandinavia, Germany and Italy in the West and the Soviet Union in the East. Geographically, they do not form any unit, and historically they are likewise divided, at least by the difference, so frequently stressed in the present study, between Old Europe, including the Balkans, and New Europe, north of the Danubian region. For these and other reasons some of those who during the last war so strongly recommended a federalization of that whole group of smaller countries, envisaged not one, but two or even three regional federations in this part of Europe.[29] But sometimes the whole of it was called a " New Europe "[30] in the political sense, emphasizing that the peace settlement after 1918 had completed the process of liberation of all these peoples from Greece to Finland.

Besides the Danubian States, the country which most definitely belongs to East-Central Europe is, of course, Poland, the largest of the whole group and occupying a key position, both geographically and historically.[31] In spite of a striking continuity in Polish history through the whole millennium of the European Age, from the tenth to the twentieth century, a continuity which even the dismemberment in the nineteenth could not destroy, there are, even in Polish historiography, two different interpretations of the Polish tradition, usually connected with the heritage of two dynasties: the Piasts and the Jagellonians.[32] In the Piast period Poland had been limited to her ethnic homelands,[33] parts of which were gradually lost to Germany. Under the Jagellonians, Poland was the centre of a federal system which temporarily included even Bohemia, Hungary, and the Rumanian principalities, and for many centuries united Poland proper, Lithuania, Ruthenia (what now is called the Ukraine and Byelorussia), and Livonia (Latvia and parts of Estonia) in one Commonwealth.

Since the restoration of that Commonwealth in a modern form proved impossible after the liberation of its whole area in 1918,[34] there arose not only the question of the political boundary between the new Poland and her former partners in the Jagellonian federation, but also the problem as to the part of Europe to which these other members of the historic Union would belong. In the case of the three Baltic republics, it was obvious that, like Poland, they were an integral part of East Central Europe, together with their northern neighbour, Finland, whose historic association with Sweden resulted in an intermediary position between the Baltic and the Scandinavian groups.[35] The case of old Ruthenia is, however, a much more difficult issue, subject to different interpretations, although one of them, which was propagated under Tsarist rule and assumed that both Little Russians (Ukrainians) and White Russians were parts of one indivisible Russian nation, seems now definitely abandoned.[36]

The Russian Revolution recognized both of these as separate nations, but soon after their declarations of independence forced upon them Communist governments which made them join the Soviet Union as constituent republics together with the Russian Federated Soviet Republic.[37] Practically dominated by the latter, they found themselves, together with it, outside a Europe which, distinct from Soviet Eurasia, consists of three parts only : Western Europe in the proper sense, the German centre, and the countries between Germany and the Soviet Union. The present control of all these countries by Soviet Russia would eventually reduce Europe to two parts : the West and Germany. If, on the contrary, the Ukraine and Byelorussia should be free from Soviet Russia, these two nations could be considered Eastern Europe proper, although their historical ties with East-Central Europe would favour their inclusion in that group.

Modern Ukrainian historiography rightly stresses the Western trends in the past of that country[38] in contradistinction to Russian history, and the same can be said with regard to Byelorussia. It is true that some Russian scholars, such as George Vernadsky, while fully aware of the distinct individuality of the Ukraine and White Russia, try to include their whole past in the general course of Russian history ;[39] but that makes the whole presentation rather artificial, the more so because Vernadsky favours at the same time the Eurasian interpretation of Russian history, which cannot be applied to the Western *Ruś*. It is equally doubtful whether federation with a Russia integrated in the European community would be the best solution of the problem of the now " submerged " Ukrainian nation.[40] But this is a question of the future, and therefore beyond the scope of historical research.

The historian can merely repeat that if and when Russia is considered part of Europe, he has to distinguish, not two nor even three, but four constituent parts of the continent, except that in the nineteenth century, and until the European War of 1914 to 1918, one of these divisions seemed non-existent, because the whole region between Germany and Russia had been absorbed by the German and Russian Empires, while the liberation of the Balkan nations from the Ottoman Empire was only beginning. Under these conditions, which even today influence the approach of many historians, it was easy to identify Central Europe with Germany and her " brilliant second ", to consider it the last outpost of Western civilization—the real Europe—and to identify the comparatively new field of Eastern European history with the history of Russia, which seemed to cover, more or less, the whole " Slavic world ".

Rejecting these misconceptions, let us consider, in conclusion, the advantages of a geographical division of European history into four sections, without giving any importance to the terms Western, West-Central, East-Central, and Eastern, which were tentatively used above.

One of the main defects of that whole terminology, and of the basic distinction between Western and Eastern Europe, lies in the impression obviously created that all of what is geographically " Eastern " is alien, or even opposed, to " Western "— that is, truly European—civilization. As a matter of fact, a closer study of the various historical regions of Europe confirms quite another impression, which first seemed paradoxical : it appears that some countries which are situated in the eastern, or at least the east-central, part of Europe have particularly close ties, cultural and even political, with the Latin West of the continent.

This is especially evident in the case of Catholic nations, whether Slavic like the Poles, Czechs or Croats, or of any other racial origin, like the Lithuanians and the Hungarians. But even nations whose Christian faith and historic tradition is Eastern, in the sense of Greek Orthodoxy, were attracted by the Latin West, particularly when exposed to the onslaught of the Asiatic East. After liberation from Ottoman, non-European domination, they showed themselves more anxious than ever to re-establish close relations with Western Europe and her culture.[41]

These relations were at the same time an escape from Russian imperialism, not only in the Balkan, but also in the Ukrainian case ; that Russian, East European imperialism, on the other hand, frequently co-operated with German imperialism, which is Western in its appearances because associated with the tradition of the Western Roman Empire, but in its essence is distinctly anti-Latin, opposed to the aspirations of Western Europe in the proper sense.

The political philosophies of Germany and Russia always had much in common,[42] were it only because each pretended to be the legitimate heir of the ancient Empire in one of its two forms. Such claims were always rejected by the Latin and Anglo-Saxon West, as well as by all countries between Germany and Russia, with the sole difference that the former seemed threatened only by one imperialism, while the latter were under a similar pressure from two sides. Even when the old imperial ideas were losing their practical significance in the era of modern nationalism, that nationalism had different features in the two pairs of European regions which seem such a challenge to geography. The liberal ideas of the Latin and Anglo-Saxon West found an enthusiastic response in the distant region of East-Central Europe, while the specifically German form of nationalism, whether idealistic or materialistic in its philosophy, deeply influenced similar trends in modern Russia.[43]

From the tenth century to the twentieth—that is, throughout the course of European history—Germany's immediate eastern neighbours, younger members of the European community, tried to promote their cultural development in direct co-operation with the Latin homelands of European civilization, without passing through a German intermediary. But as soon as Muscovite Russia developed her even younger power east of them, a co-operation was inaugurated between Germany and that new power[44] which might be considered either a fourth European region, in the geographical and historical order, or an extra-European force extending far into Asia.

The persistent purpose of that co-operation was the encirclement and isolation, and eventually the complete elimination, if
necessary through partition, of all the nations which separated
Germany from Russia, and formed the real eastern bulwark of
European civilization. From that point of view, it is interesting
to recall that the first German-Russian alliance, concluded as
early as 1490, was answered as early as 1500 by a first alliance
of the whole Jagellonian system—Poland, Lithuania, Bohemia
and Hungary—with France and Venice.[45] Fifteen years later,
a first Congress of Vienna tried in vain to reconcile the two parts
of Central Europe on a basis of equality,[46] and in 1815 another,
much better-known Congress in the same city sanctioned the
disappearance of the eastern, non-German part, which remained
divided between two German powers, Russia and Turkey. After
the Paris Peace Conference of 1919, that forgotten region of
Europe reappeared in the form of a dozen free and independent
countries, but only to face the persistent hostility of both
Germany and Russia, equally opposed to such an organization
of the " balkanized " *Zwischen-Europa* which separated them
like a *cordon sanitaire*.[47]

In one of his provocative books,[48] David J. Dallin has
compared three maps of that region : the first showed it as a
group of free nations, closely connected with a friendly and
democratic France which influenced them culturally in the
Western spirit, but was too distant either to threaten or to protect them effectively; the second and the third showed the same
area dominated during the last war by Germany, and after that
by Russia, the two powers which had tried to divide it again
between themselves in the years of the Nazi-Soviet co-operation.

The history of the balance of power system, to which the
whole political history of Europe is so frequently reduced,
remains incomplete as long as the crucial problem of the second

VII. THE DUALISM OF CENTRAL EUROPE

Central Europe, the third of four basic regions of Europe, is ignored. But even with that problem included, the history of the balance of power system is not the whole political history of Europe; this was not the only system of Europe's organization. A constitution based upon the idea of universalism was also tried in that European Age, which was inclined to identify Europe with the universe and which, to a certain extent, really made Europe the centre of universal history. But the whole issue of universalism versus balance of power requires a preliminary discussion, not only of the geographical, but also of the chronological divisions of European history.

CHAPTER VIII

The Chronological Divisions:
(a) The Middle Ages and The Renaissance

The Chronological Divisions:
(a) The Middle Ages and The Renaissance

THE CONVENTIONAL divisions of European history into chrono-logical periods are almost as inadequate as the conventional divisions of the European continent into geographical regions. And they are so for similar reasons. One of them is the relative character of the names which are given to the traditional periods: ancient, mediaeval and modern, as well as to the usual territorial sections: western, central, and eastern. But there is another reason, common to both inadequacies. The divisions of European history, whether geographical or chonological, have been drafted without taking into consideration the problem of the limits of European history both in space and in time.

That statement needs to be explained. As far as the territorial divisions are concerned, the greatest difficulty in establishing them resulted from the fact, so frequently overlooked, that the historical European community cannot be simply identified with geographical Europe, because the frontiers of that community, especially in the East, were not fixed once for all, but moving back and forth. That same fact must be taken into serious consideration before a decision is made concerning the division into chronological periods, which ought to correspond to the historical evolution of all members of the European com-munity. On the one hand, any division based upon the develop-ment of only a certain part of that community, for instance the Western, would hardly meet the requirements of general

European history. On the other hand, it would be a hopeless undertaking to look for a division which would cover the history of territories which in the given period were not really part of historical Europe, but under the impact of extra-European forces. Such an approach to the problem of chronological periods, involved as it seems to be, is at the same time a helpful test of whether or not the determination of Europe's boundaries, based upon different considerations, is in full agreement with the reality of the historical process.

It is much easier to explain, or rather to recall, that the chronological limits of European history as a whole—the middle of the tenth century, when the making of Europe was completed, and the middle of the twentieth, when the European Age had definitely passed—offer entirely new starting points for the periodization of European history. If the problem of chronological divisions is thus reduced to the task of sub-dividing the millennium of the European Age into a few successive phases of development, the necessary revision of the conventional scheme will be reduced in turn to two basic questions.

The first of these questions concerns the Middle Ages, the second modern history, because the European Age, as defined above, includes a large part of what is usually called mediaeval history together with the following centuries, usually called modern, which lead us to our own times. What is needed is, therefore, a reinterpretation of these two concepts, which seem so familiar and yet remain rather vague and controversial, whether we consider the content of either of them or their mutual relationship.

Especially vague and controversial is the interpretation of the Middle Ages, and yet it is the necessary introduction to any study of chronological periods, since the conventional division has placed that period in the very centre—the " middle "— of all history, subject to the criticism of those who consider it a " dark age " between two much brighter periods.[1] This one-sided attitude, which can be traced back to the prejudice, largely philological, of many humanists, and to a much more violent bias during the age of the so-called Enlightenment, has now been definitely abandoned, along with the equally one-sided idealization of everything " mediaeval " which characterized the period of Romanticism. But what seems equally outmoded is the idea that the ten centuries from the fifth to the fifteenth, all included under the one name " mediaeval ", really were one age and can be considered a homogeneous whole. The striking difference between the earlier of these centuries, some of them really " dark ",[2] and the later ones, which left us a durable cultural heritage, made the historians look for a division within the conventional Middle Ages even before the question of a general revision of the periods of European history was raised.

The lasting, uncontroversial result of these investigations was the discovery of various " renaissances " in the course of the mediaeval period. Since the Middle Ages and the Renaissance at the beginning of the next period, the modern, had long been considered completely different from, and opposed to, each other, such a discovery was almost revolutionary. Furthermore, not only the concept of the Middle Ages, but another rather vague and controversial term also had to be reinterpreted,[3] once it was admitted that there had been in European history, not just one Renaissance, a unique phenomenon, but several more or less analogous periods of cultural " rebirth ", in the sense of both a revival of ancient tradition and a new creative vitality.

The question remained, however, as to which of these successive " renaissances " was the decisive turning point from the " dark " pre-mediaeval centuries to the Middle Ages proper, with all their constructive achievements. There might well be a certain amount of hesitancy in the choice between the first, the Carolingian Renaissance, early in the ninth century, and the renaissance which followed towards the end of the tenth century, sometimes called the Ottonian, but largely attributable to the Cluny movement.[4] The chaos which intervened in Europe between the two revivals would be a serious argument for stressing the second ; moreover, all that has been said above about the beginning of European history and its geographical extension points to the decisive significance of the tenth century.

But there is an additional argument in favour of the thesis that a new period—the first of the European Age and therefore hard to call " mediaeval ", although it corresponds to the Middle Ages in their traditional meaning—began precisely towards the end of the tenth century. A really important historical period must have not only well-justified chronological limits marking both its beginning and its end, but also a leading idea, typical of its content. Now, as far as the Middle Ages are concerned, it is not difficult to discover, under the rather unfortunate and meaningless name given to that period, a great idea which was in fact the political philosophy and the inspiration of all truly mediaeval generations. It is the idea of universalism.

In theory this was supposed to be the universality of " one world ", as we would say today. In practice, it could not be more than a universality within the limits of the part of the world which was known to those who conceived the idea of universalism. That part of the world was, of course, Europe as an historical community, identical in these centuries with Christendom, so that the greatest representative of mediaeval universalism, in whose individual mind the synthesis of the mediaeval mind was achieved, has been rightly called a " citizen of Christendom ".[5]

Even in these limits the idea of universalism could not be born before the European community was finally formed. But as soon as historical Europe was " made ", its most prominent representatives fully realized that it had to be organized : Christendom must become the *Respublica Christiana*, based upon diversity in unity. Why it was to be from the outset, and to remain until Dante's vision of a universal *monarchia*, a unity under the leadership of two universal powers, Pope *and* Emperor ; why, in the new Christian Republic, the ghost of a defunct Empire was evoked—that is a separate problem which, briefly mentioned above,[6] will be discussed later. Here it will suffice to say that the first period of European history, which began with the rise of universalism, consequently ended with the disintegration of " mediaeval " unity : it lasted as long as the predominance of that idea.

There was, indeed, no universalism in the so-called modern period of European history, which in the usual interpretation is supposed to follow immediately after the mediaeval. Therefore, in all discussions of the chronological division of history the question of the dividing line between these two periods has received a well-deserved attention. But two mistakes are usually made in that connection. The first is one more result of the old prejudice against the " dark " Middle Ages which are opposed to the brightness of a new era of progress. The contrast between the two successive periods has been sometimes over-emphasized to such an extent that the chronological unity and uninterrupted continuity of all European history seemed to vanish.

This error included the misconception that there must be a clear cut, a decisive turning point, separating mediaeval from modern history ; and this is, of course, the same mistake as the one made until recently in dividing ancient and mediaeval history by stressing the date of this or that individual year. The confusing consequences of such a method, typical of the whole conventional division of history according to Cellarius's pattern, are particularly obvious in the case of the end of the

Middle Ages. For the date originally given : 1453, the fall of Constantinople, was and frequently is replaced by a few other equally arbitrary dates of which only one, the date of the invention of the printing machine around 1450, approaches the original choice, while the others : 1492—the discovery of America, 1517—the Lutheran Reformation, or 1519—the election of Charles V, move the dividing line from the middle of the fifteenth to the beginning of the sixteenth century. [7]

All these dates have serious arguments in their favour, but this only shows that there *is* no single date separating the two basic periods ; on the contrary, they are connected, in the uninterrupted course of European history, by a period of transition similar to that which preceded the beginning of the European Age. Instead of a striking contrast between " mediaeval " and " modern " times, there appears to have been a gradual change which had already begun before 1453 and was not yet completed in 1519. That slow evolution went through so many consecutive phases, and lasted so long, that it seemed advisable to consider the transition from the first to the last period of European history as a period in itself. And it is easy to suggest a suitable name for this period, since it corresponds to the rise and decline of the Renaissance, the cultural " rebirth " to which that designation is specifically attached ; meaning, of course, not merely a new artistic style, but a new way of life with new political conceptions.

The bisecting of the Renaissance period is one of the worst shortcomings of the usual division of history, and since that period does consist of two parts, each of which used to be included in one of the conventional periods, two equally important questions must be answered : which part of " mediaeval " history and which part of " modern " history—to use the terminology of our text-books—really belongs to the history of the Renaissance ?

As we attempt to answer the first question the usual danger of over-stressing the contrast between two successive periods immediately presents itself. That there was no absolute contrast between the Middle Ages and the Renaissance has been best explained by Etienne Gilson.[8] Renaissance elements in mediaeval culture, which he exemplifies in the famous story of Abélard and Héloïse, are so evident that, in addition to the various " renaissances " which preceded the Middle Ages in the strict sense, at least one more renaissance must be admitted, occurring right in the middle of these ages : that of the twelfth century, so well described by Charles Haskins.[9]

Furthermore, it is hardly necessary to state that, again, it would be vain to look for any single date which would stand out as a landmark between the real Middle Ages and the Renaissance *par excellence*. Proceeding through elimination, the historian must first realize which centuries are undoubtedly on one or the other side of the border which he wants to determine with as much precision as possible.

There is no question that the thirteenth century is typically mediaeval ; only an artificial exaggeration of the " genetic " method could trace the Renaissance so far back as this.[10] Such an approach would obliterate the Middle Ages altogether and give the impression that the whole course of European history was nothing but an almost uninterrupted series of renaissance movements. It is, however, almost equally certain that the fifteenth century was no longer really mediaeval. It might be called, with Huizinga, the " autumn " or the " vanishing " of the Middle Ages,[11] but, as a matter of fact, it was already typical of the new era.

This is not true only because Renaissance art was already flourishing in Italy. Since the Renaissance is not considered here merely from the point of view of art, nor from that of any individual country, such an argument would be insufficient.

But the new conception of the state as something like a work of art, which represented a distinct departure from the traditional interpretation, had already appeared in that century outside Italy where the Swiss scholar Karl Burckhardt found in this conception the first test of a general change.[12] And when Ludwig v. Pastor decided to study the general history of the Papacy " from the end of the Middle Ages ", he had to treat the second half of the fifteenth century as an integral part of his field and the first half as an indispensable introduction.[13]

It was precisely that first half of the *Quatrocento* which saw the unavoidable failure of a last attempt to revive mediaeval universalism by developing, more than in any other period of ecclesiastical history, the machinery of universal Councils, and by using a third universal power besides the Papacy and the Empire : the *studium generale*, the Universities.[14] The complete disappointment in which that great experience issued— what its foremost historian, Noël Valois, has rightly called " the religious crisis of the fifteenth century "[15]—is the best evidence that the age of universalism had definitely passed. And this was precisely, as explained above, the Middle Ages in their real meaning.

The obvious conclusion would, therefore, be that the passing of the Middle Ages took place between the thirteenth and the fifteenth—that is, in the fourteenth—centuries. But in which part of it ? There are reasonable grounds for arguing that it was at the beginning of that century. The typically mediaeval Crusades seemed to have ended with the fall of Acre, in 1291, and a few years later the Ottoman Turks started the offensive of Islam.[16] The authority of the Papacy, after defeating the Empire in the preceding century, suffered in turn its deepest humiliation in 1303 from the King of France, under whose influence it came after the transfer to Avignon two years later. And the bold ideas expressed in the lifetime of the same generation by Marsilius of Padua seem to indicate that the decline of mediaeval universalism was in fact the beginning of the much deeper religious crisis leading to the Protestant Reformation.[17]

But it can be answered that there was a crusading movement at least until Nicopolis, in 1396—the date recently stressed by S. A. Atiya;[18] that the Avignon period, which saw, under John XXII, a new, typically mediaeval conflict between Papacy and Empire was not at all a " Babylonian exile " of the Church, which, as proved by G. Mollat,[19] did not in any sense lose its truly universal authority; and that there was no really dangerous heresy extending its influence from country to country, directly leading to Hussite and indirectly to Protestant doctrines, before John Wycliff—that is, before the later part of the century.

It is, therefore, rather towards the end of the fourteenth century that the decisive turn must be placed, and there is even an individual date which is of unusual significance in itself, and still more significant if various events which surround it are taken into consideration. It was in 1378, one year after the return of Gregory XI from Avignon to Rome, that the election of his successor, Urban VI, provoked the Great Western Schism; at the very time when the chances of reuniting Western and Eastern Christendom were most favourable,[20] this conflict destroyed the unity of the Church even in the West; lasting, in two returns, for seventy years, and opposing to each other the authorities of Pope and Council, it made any constructive reform of the Church impossible and thus prepared the religious revolution of the sixteenth century.

In the same year 1378 occurred the death of Charles IV, who had tried, not without success, to restore the authority of the Holy Emperor;[21] his son Sigismund made this attempt in vain[22] after a schism had taken place in the Empire parallel to the schism in the Church. A twofold crisis, with three popes at the same time, each recognized in different parts of Christendom, and three rivals in the contest for the imperial crown, could not but result in the complete disintegration of mediaeval unity.

The crisis centred, of course, in Italy and Germany, but the Western Kingdoms, also affected by the schism, were simultaneously undergoing the protracted crisis of the Hundred Years' War. It is true that this war had started at an earlier date and was practically interrupted when the papal and imperial schisms reached their climax. But there is a profound difference between the two phases of the war. In the earlier phase it was a typically mediaeval conflict : a dynastic rivalry on feudal grounds. When England resumed the struggle under a new dynasty which had no possible claim to the French crown, the issue became the existence of France as a separate nation within a European community already completely divided into individual national states. The great change which occurred in Western Europe at the transition from the later fourteenth to the early fifteenth century becomes evident if we compare Froissart's story of the first part of the Hundred Years' War[23] with the records of the trial of Joan of Arc :[24] the trial itself seems typically mediaeval, and so are the " mysteries " in the life of the victim,[25] but she is at the same time the first representative of a nationalism which already has distinctly " modern " features, including the participation of the people in a great patriotic movement.

Similar features appear simultaneously in the development of Polish and Czech nationalism in opposition to a new wave of German expansion. There is, indeed, a difference between the two Slavic movements : Poland remained completely Catholic, although her Teutonic opponent was a religious Order, the Knights of the Cross, whom she eventually defeated ; the Hussite movement, on the other hand, combined nationalism with heresy and issued in failure. But in any case the parallel and synchronized developments in the Western and the Eastern part of the European community are striking. And they appear even more so if the events which culminated in the battle of Tannenberg (Grunwald, 1410)[26] and in the trial of John Huss (1415), followed by the Hussite Wars, are traced back to their origins.

In the Czech case such a study leads to a reform movement contemporaneous with, and influenced by, John Wycliff's.[27] In Poland it points to a date very near to 1378, and almost as significant. The treaty of Krewo in 1385, prepared through negotiations which started in 1377,[28] created the Polish-Lithuanian Union of the following year and, as explained above, included in the European community both the Lithuanians, the last European heathens converted to Catholicism, and the Ruthenians of White Russia and the Ukraine, who remained Greek Orthodox but soon appeared interested in the projects of religious reunion.[29]

That great change in the Eastern European situation deeply affected the whole Baltic region, where the federation of the Scandinavian Kingdoms in the Kalmar Union of 1397, another check of German imperialism, entered into close relations with the Polish-Lithuanian federal system.[30] But the latter, which a few years after Krewo extended to the Black Sea region, had an additional significance for Europe as a whole, as a bulwark against the danger of Asiatic invasions, a danger which greatly increased in the same critical years towards the end of the fourteenth century. The first great Ottoman victory on European soil in the battle of Adrianople—already Turkey's capital —in 1371,[31] another more famous defeat of the Serbs in 1389, and the conquest of Bulgaria four years later, are decisive dates in the history of the whole Balkan peninsula, and the appearance of Tamerlane was a challenge to both North-Eastern and South-Eastern Europe.[32]

But here the crucial problem presents itself, whether the end of the fourteenth century—the years around and soon after 1378—really was a decisive turning point, a chronological limit between two periods, for the whole European continent in the geographical sense. Tamerlane's invasion, which was checked at the Lithuanian border in spite of the victory of his lieutenant in the battle of the Vorskla (1399), had, of course, repercussions in Muscovite Russia, still under the overlordship of other Tartar Khans,[33] but it did not have, in Russian history, the catastrophic significance of the Mongol conquest in the middle of the thirteenth century. On the other hand, that new Asiatic intervention in European affairs indirectly preserved the Byzantine Empire for about fifty years, through the defeat inflicted upon the Turks in the battle of Angora, 1402.

The conclusion is clear. For Europe as an historic community, a great period called the Mediaeval ended with the fourteenth century. But that division could hardly be applied to the history of Great Russia, where the significant period of Tartar domination had started one hundred and fifty years before and did not end until one hundred years later.[34] The Russia which developed outside the mediaeval European world also remained outside the crisis of the Western schism, which reached only as far as the eastern frontier of the Polish-Lithuanian federation. That crisis had indeed its repercussions as far as Byzantium,[35] which never ceased to be part of historic Europe. But the Eastern Roman Empire was already so dependent on the Asiatic forces which encircled Constantinople that, politically, the events of the late fourteenth century proved less decisive there than elsewhere in Europe, although culturally Byzantium, so far as with greatly reduced territory it survived these critical events, entered with Western Europe the new period called the Renaissance.[36]

The Renaissance period lasted, of course, much longer than

until the fall of Constantinople in 1453, or until any of the dates around 1500 to which a great chronological division of European history is usually ascribed. As soon as we replace these conventional frontiers between mediaeval and modern Europe by a whole transition period between the two, which includes more than a century of the traditional Middle Ages, we have to consider the additional problem as to how much of the traditional " modern " period really belongs to the Renaissance Age. No single date comparable in importance to 1378 can be found to offer an adequate solution. But the dates of certain events which correspond to those at the beginning of the period point very definitely to the second half of the sixteenth century.

The religious division of Western Christendom, fore-shadowed by the schism of 1378, became final when the Protestant Reformation was recognized as an accomplished fact in agreements such as those of Augsburg in 1555, of Warsaw in 1573,[37] or of Nantes in 1598. During these same years of transition, the Catholic Counter-Reformation—or rather, Restoration—through a clear determination of the traditional doctrine and an improvement of ecclesiastical organization, was accomplished by the Council of Trent, and after the conclusion of the third session of this Council in 1563, gradually became effective in all countries which remained faithful to Rome.

In a European community thus divided in religious matters, formerly the main element of its unity, the process of secular-ization, begun during the Renaissance, also reached completion, especially in the field of politics. It is true that during the sixteenth century the idea of completely separating politics from ethics, so strongly recommended by Macchiavelli at the be-ginning of that century,[38] was already being put into practice to an unprecedented extent. But it was only at the end of the century, and even more during the following period of the

Thirty Years' War, that religion was used merely as a pretext for armed conflicts between the individual sovereign powers.

Not even the powers which remained Catholic respected the universal authority of the Holy See, and, more momentous even than the death of Charles IV in 1378, the abdication of Charles V in 1555 represented a further and final step in the disintegration of the Empire.[39] The fiction of its supranational universality could no longer be maintained, since the territory which at least nominally remained under the Emperor's authority was now reduced to, and identical with, Germany. Even Bohemia's exceptional position within that German Empire did not last longer than until 1620.[40]

In spite of dynastic ties, the Spanish part of that which, under Charles V, had seemed to be a modernized universal state of Western Christendom was now an entirely separate body politic, and what is sometimes called—not without exaggeration—the Spanish predominance in Europe,[41] likewise ended with the sixteenth century. In that same century, the process of discoveries and overseas colonization was completed, so far as it was a search for the best ways to India and a preparation for the inclusion of the Western Hemisphere in the European sphere of influence. That whole process which lasted about two hundred years, and not merely the date of 1492, separates, as one of the most striking aspects of the Renaissance period, the mediaeval world from the modern.

Accomplished first under Spanish and Portuguese leadership, the process of discovery turned, towards the end of the sixteenth century, into an entirely new era of colonial expansion through English and Dutch initiative. The date of 1588, the destruction of the Great Armada, is a well-known turning point in that respect, and it is significant that Spain lost her leading position only eight years after depriving Portugal for two generations of her independence. Neither of the two Iberian countries was ever to regain its great power position, typical of the Renaissance period, while the rise of Elizabethan England inaugurated the new rôle of the Anglo-Saxon element in both the old European and the new colonial worlds of the following centuries.

Before this great change became fully apparent, it was France which, throughout her *Grand Siècle*, seemed to dominate the European continent from its western corner. But even under Louis XIV she could not balance what remained of the Habsburg influence without building up a system of alliances in the eastern part of Europe, based upon the great changes which were likewise appearing there towards the end of the sixteenth century.

It is no accident that French policy showed a real interest in Baltic problems and Scandinavian-Polish relations for the first time at the Congress of Stettin, in 1570.[42] Just a year before, at the Lublin Diet of 1569,[43] the Polish-Lithuanian Commonwealth had been finally constituted. The federal system, started, at the beginning of the Renaissance period, in 1385, was thus completed, only to be implemented in the religious sphere by the Union of Brest, 1596,[44] that one compensation for the losses of the Catholic Church in Western Europe. At the same time, however, the territorial expansion of this federation under Polish leadership ended with the addition of the southern part of the formerly German State of Livonia, its northern part going to the new Baltic power of Sweden.[45]

The dynastic union between Poland and Sweden under the Vasas seemed to accomplish, in 1587, what had been planned by the founders of the Jagellonian and Kalmar Unions two hundred years before. As a matter of fact, that date became a turning point for an entirely different reason : just at the turn of the century, the election of 1587 resulted in a Polish-Swedish war, contrary to the traditions and interests of both countries.[46] For Poland, the following century was to be a Hundred Years'

War, which is the real cause of the decline of that great power of the Renaissance period ; Sweden's new great power rôle was to affect general European politics in an unexpected way at the very beginning of modern times.

This time, contrary to the situation at the end of the real Middle Ages, it might seem as if Muscovite Russia and the Ottoman Empire, the two outsiders of the historic European community, still excluded from it in the political conceptions of the age of Henry IV, passed simultaneously with the other European countries from one period of their history to another. Russia certainly passed through an exceptionally critical " time of troubles "[47] between the extinction of the Rurik dynasty in 1598 and the election of the first Romanov in 1613. And the rise of the Ottoman Empire, corresponding to the Renaissance period, was almost suddenly interrupted after the death in 1566 of the last in a brilliant line of successive sultans, Suleiman the Magnificent, and the assassination of his last and most prominent vizir, Mohammed Sokolli, in 1579,[48] soon after the first major defeat of the Turks at Lepanto (1571), and not too long before the first unfavourable treaty with a Christian power, concluded at Zsitva Torok in 1606.

It is, however, significant that in both cases the really decisive turn in the history of the country and the repercussion on general European history did not come until one hundred years later. Russia's " time of troubles " was, after all, mainly an internal crisis, deeply rooted in the earlier reign of Ivan the Terrible but not leading to any basic reform, while the foreign invasion, with Poland and Sweden acting separately and in opposition to each other, was merely incidental, contrary to the exaggerated interpretation in the Russian tradition.[49] The real change which made Muscovy a great Empire, influencing the destinies of all Europe, came only with Peter the Great. As to Turkey's decline, it was not realized for a long time by her

Christian neighbours, who continued to be threatened by her invasions until Sobieski's victory before Vienna in 1683[50] reversed the situation, so that the Ottoman Empire was threatened in turn, from the Carlovitz Treaty in 1699, by a reconquest of its European possessions, if not by partition projects typical of the modern phase of the Eastern Question.

But with the exception of Russia and Turkey, both of which remained isolated from the great European trends of the Renaissance, Reformation, and Counter-Reformation, as they had been isolated from the developments of the so-called Middle Ages, European history of the two centuries between the later fourteenth and the later sixteenth has a distinct unity, thanks chiefly to these cultural trends which created their styles of art as well as their climates of thought.

Politically, the same two centuries are characterized by a process of disintegration which clearly distinguishes them from the preceding period of universalism and corresponds to the spiritual division of Christendom. All this is too important, and lasted too long, merely to be considered a transition between two periods ; the Renaissance, in the largest sense of that term, ought to be recognized in itself as an important period of European history, its critical period, followed by a third one which is the core of what is usually called modern history.

CHAPTER IX

The Chronological Divisions:
(*b*) Modern and Contemporary History

CHAPTER IX

The Chronological Divisions:
(b) Modern and Contemporary History

IN HIS recent " Valedictory " to the *Journal of Modern History*, Bernadotte E. Schmitt recalled[1] that when he began his studies, the American Civil War and the Franco-German War of 1870–1871 were still vivid in men's minds. The period from 1871 or 1878 to 1914 was then " contemporary " history, just as the period from 1919 to 1938—or rather, to the present—is today. A similar experience has been undergone by earlier generations of historians, to whom practically the whole nineteenth century seemed " contemporary ", and the phenomenon will persist as long as history is studied and written. The very term " contemporary history ", whether applied to European or to any other history, is, therefore, even more questionable than the other conventional names given to the main chronological divisions : it is not only relative, as they all are, but completely subjective, continuously changing its real meaning, and even self-contradictory, since, after all, history is what happened in the past, and not what is happening contemporarily, i.e. in the present.

This being so, the question might be asked, whether there is any such thing as contemporary history, and whether it is necessary to consider it here as one of the possible periods of history, with a view to deciding what part of it, if any, belongs to the European Age, and to understanding its relationship with the preceding, definitely European period which is called " modern ". The real problem is, however, not so much one more point of mere terminology as it is the question of finding a clarifying reinterpretation for what is usually designated as " contemporary " history. And this is a vital problem, since it is precisely that " contemporary " period which arouses the greatest interest among the average students of history : they are always inclined to concentrate almost exclusively on the most recent developments, while more and more of the passing events are, so to speak, gradually put in storage in the department which continues to be called modern history, although in the contemporary consciousness it is not really " modern " at all.

It is not difficult to discover that contemporary history is nothing but the period in which we happen to live. Since it is an obviously unfinished period, it is practically impossible to name it—hence the vague designation usually applied—or even to fix its proper place in the course of human evolution. For with regard to any generation of historians, it has hardly been possible to do more than to find out when *their* contemporary period began, so that it might be distinguished, as part of a new unit, from the preceding one. But the situation becomes particularly involved, if during the lifetime of one generation a decisive turn of history closes one period and opens another. And that is precisely what has happened to us.

For those who still remember the world before 1914 which William C. Bullitt so vividly contrasts to the whole climate of the following decades,[2] it is clear that in their youth they lived in a period of history entirely different from the present : two successive periods with little in common have, therefore, been contemporary for them. Furthermore, our generation has also experienced the difficulty of establishing precise limits between various chronological periods : it is, for instance, not easy to say whether the year of decisive change really was 1914 or whether it was 1939 instead. The choice depends on the interpretation of the two great wars fought in our time, and the two decades between them. Were there really two wars, basically different from each other, or are they both parts of one war, another " Thirty Years' War ", or " the War of the Twentieth Century " ?[3] Were the intermediate years a short but real period of peace, or were they only a " Twenty Years' Truce " ?[4] Whatever the answer to such questions might be, it is obvious that the last effort of reorganizing and saving Europe during these years of peace or armistice unfortunately failed, and that together with the war years which preceded and followed them, they ended the European Age.

Nevertheless the beginning of that end must have started long before. The passing from the European to the Atlantic Age must have lasted, as shown above,[5] much longer. In spite of what we have called the accelerated rhythm of history, the change was too drastic to be completed within twenty or thirty years. On the contrary it took, as is usual in such cases, a whole period of transition, precisely the period which throughout its gradual extensions continued to be called " contemporary ", but for us is no longer contemporary at all.

Before studying the precise limits of that period, which obviously must now receive a new interpretation, it might be pointed out that the designation " contemporary ", if it is to be used with any real sense, must now be given to the events following the great crisis of 1914-1945—not to the end of the European, but to the beginning of the Atlantic Age, or rather, of the first period of that new age. It will be the task of the historians of the future to characterize in retrospect and possibly to name that period. For the present generation it is not yet history, and its study, urgent as it is, does not yet belong to the field of historical science. It is rather political science in the largest sense of that term, including both the new science of " international relations ", dealing with the problems which are now of paramount importance, and the study of political, cultural and economic conditions in the individual countries of the world of today, in which it is increasingly difficult to consider any of them in isolation.

Returning after that brief digression to history proper, we must return at the same time to problems already touched in the chapter on the end of the European Age. What remains to be done is to indicate with more chronological precision when the so-called modern period of European history turned into a period of transition in which the disintegrating European community temporarily coexisted with an Atlantic community in the making. This is a problem which is certainly as important as the determination of the relationship between the so-called Middle Ages and the Renaissance.

As far as modern history is concerned, it has been shown in the preceding chapter how that period of European history started about one hundred years later than is usually admitted. The suggestion that it shall be considered to have begun not before the end of the sixteenth century makes its designation as " modern " somewhat less shocking and confusing. But what really matters is, again, not so much the name as the distinctive character of the period. And that appears most clearly if the European state system, typical of the " modern " centuries, is studied against the background of its earlier origin.

That origin cannot be found except in mediaeval universalism, which seemed to disappear completely during the crisis of the Renaissance period. But if it is obvious that the two universal powers of the Middle Ages, the Papacy and the Empire, had lost their political leadership, it is equally true that the idea of European unity embodied in the conception of a Christian " Republic ", or rather, " Commonwealth " (as the Latin word *Respublica* is best translated), survived even in modern Europe. It lacked, however, any concrete form of organization, and its very content underwent basic changes under the influence of a new political conception which originated during the Renaissance period in one of the European countries, to become in the following period the unwritten constitution of the continent.

Whatever we may think of the authenticity and seriousness of the plan for the organization of Europe formulated by Henry IV (or rather, by his minister, Sully)[6] at the beginning of the seventeenth century, it proves that Europe's political philosophy still took for granted the existence of the *République Chrétienne* and its solidarity against the Ottoman danger. But more than in similar projects and negotiations of the past, the idea of a joint action against a common, non-Christian and non-European enemy was a mere pretext covering the real rivalry between Christian and European powers. The persistence of the old, mediaeval idea can be studied in contemporary sources throughout the whole seventeenth century,[7] at least until its last triumph in what might be called the Crusade of 1683 and the Holy League of the following year. But even the continuing fight against the rapidly declining Ottoman Empire was soon to change its character so completely that the next generation, that of Voltaire, spoke no longer of a Christian, but merely of a half-secularized " Great Republic ".[8] And all those who praise that idea even in its new form must also praise its new basic conception : the famous balance of power.

The origin of that conception is now well known. In American historiography, Ernest W. Nelson has recently explained[9] how modern balance of power politics started in the relations among the five leading Italian states not later than about 1450 and continued throughout the period of the Italian wars in the later fifteenth century and in the first half of the sixteenth, until 1559. And since examples similar to those which he gives on his suggestive chart could be pointed out also in the course of the preceding one hundred years, when attempts at the domination of Italy by the Viscontis of Milan or by King Ladislaus of Naples were opposed by the other states of the peninsula,[10] it can be said without exaggeration that the system developed in Italy precisely during the whole Renaissance period. In the following period, as Nelson continues, the theatre having widened, the balance-of-power system, while losing its importance in an Italy completely dominated by foreign countries, became European, determining international relations on the whole continent.

The question immediately arises whether the political control of Italy by outsiders was not the consequence of a system under which, as Nelson observed, " tranquillity is not to be expected ", and one political crisis followed after the other. But leaving for a later moment the discussion of the advantages and disadvantages of the balance of power, let us consider first which powers tried to establish it on the wider scene of Europe before it was applied to the world at large.

In modern European history or, as explained above,[11] in the centuries which followed the Renaissance transition, the decline of Spain was accompanied by the rapid rise of two other typically Western powers : France and England. For reasons similar to those which caused the sixteenth to be called a century of Spanish predominance, many historians speak of a French predominance in the seventeenth century and of British predominance in the eighteenth century.[12] And it is certainly true that both kingdoms, extending their colonial empires in these centuries, combined that overseas expansion, as Spain had done, with a growing influence in all European affairs, not only in war and diplomacy, but also in culture and political philosophy ; the form of government which seems typical of these two centuries of European history, a more or less " enlightened " absolutism,[13] was certainly of French and English origin, and so were the new trends which were in opposition to its abuses.

Nevertheless, the very idea of the complete predominance of any single power in modern Europe is one of those over-simplifications from which our interpretation of history suffers so frequently. Not even under Louis XIV did France really achieve such a leadership or domination of Europe, and England never attempted it. On the contrary, she only proved anxious to oppose such a rôle on the part of any other power, particularly of France, were it even at the price of a modern " Hundred Years' War ",[14] and it was precisely in British foreign policy that the maintenance of the European balance of power became a permanent rule.[15]

First directed against possible French ambitions, the ex-aggerated fear of which was to influence Britain's policy until the very end of the European Age and frequently to mislead it, the defence of the balance of power was also used (though not always in time) against other states whenever, in British opinion, that balance was threatened. And it was precisely during the centuries of an apparent French or British predominance, practically limited to Western Europe, that a new great power rose in Eastern Europe : the power of Russia.

In order that the tremendous importance of this fact for modern European history may be realized, two points must receive special attention. First, it ought to be remembered that, like Turkey, new Muscovite Russia had started, not as an Eastern European, but as an extra-European state, outside the " Christian Republic " of a vanishing past. If Muscovite Russia became part of the modern state system, it was not so much because of a rather slow and superficial cultural Europeanization as because, in contradistinction to the declining Ottoman Empire, it became militarily so strong that all of Europe had now to reckon with it.

That was, however, not immediately realized, except, of course, by Russia's neighbours. And this leads us to the second important point. Throughout the seventeenth century, while Turkey's power, only temporarily revived by the Köprülü vizirs,[16] was largely overrated, the rise of Russia was not only underestimated, but remained almost unobserved, suddenly to appear in all its significance after the amazing victory of Poltava in 1709. Yet the achievements of Peter the Great, whose real greatness is one of the most controversial issues in Russian history and historiography,[17] would have been hardly possible without the growth of Russia under the first Romanovs. The country not only made a rapid recovery after the " Time of Troubles " and completed the conquest of Siberia as far as the Pacific and the Chinese border,[18] but interfered in turn with Poland's internal troubles in the middle of the century. By doing so Moscow not only regained her earlier conquests, which had been lost in 1618, but obtained most of the Ukraine, including Kiev[19]—a decisive step in uniting " all the Russias " under Great-Russian control.

The changes in both the West and the East deeply affected Central Europe. But in connection with the basic dualism of that region of the continent, the consequences in either of its main sections must be studied separately. The rise of France contributed necessarily to the continuing decline of the German Empire. It was her participation in the last phase of the Thirty Years' War which, more than Sweden's merely temporary impact, made the Treaty of Westphalia of 1648 so disastrous for the Imperial power and prestige, and thus a landmark in European history.

Among the many individual states which continued to be united within the Holy Roman Empire only nominally, the monarchy of the Austrian Habsburgs remained a big power, not so much because the Imperial crown remained with that dynasty as because the hereditary lands of the Habsburgs, together with their non-German Kingdoms—Bohemia within the Empire and Hungary outside it—constituted a large territorial unit, particularly after the reconquest of what had been lost to the Turks. But what was an entirely new feature in the political structure of Europe was the rise of the Hohenzollern monarchy.

This has been called the rise of Brandenburg-Prussia,[20] because a possession outside the Empire, the eastern part of Prussia, not freed from Polish suzerainty until 1657, was soon to give its name to the new big power. As Ferdinand Schevill has recently shown,[21] it was the " Great Elector " of Branden-burg who started the rise of his electorate from modest beginnings, in 1640 ; but when his grandson assumed the royal title, he called himself king of Prussia, and it was only then, in 1701, that (as in the case of his ally Peter the Great) the other powers became aware that something had been changed in the traditional European state system. It was only in the eighteenth century that Britain and also France, which was slow to realize that the Hohenzollerns rather than the Habsburgs were to be her most dangerous German opponents, gradually understood Prussia's importance in balance of power politics. But here again the change must be traced back to the preceding century, just as in the case of Russia.

The consequences of Russia's expansion were first and chiefly experienced in the eastern section of Central Europe—that is, in the Polish Commonwealth. The new power in Eastern Europe was created not so much through, and because of, an " urge to the sea " (which is hardly apparent in the seventeenth century, except in Asia)[22] as by a steady advance and pressure in the western direction, which in the eighteenth century also remained the main drive of Russian imperialism, with the elimination of the Polish barrier through complete control or partition as its primary objective.

As long as Poland, although gradually losing her big power status, continued to exist, the Western powers neglected the whole issue. They would become alarmed only when Russia advanced in the direction of the Baltic and the Black Sea—first steps in the direction of the Atlantic and the Mediterranean. Only when Russian forces, disregarding Poland's sovereignty and neutrality, began to appear on the battlefields of Germany in the European wars of the eighteenth century did it become obvious that Moscow's aggressive policy against Poland during most of the preceding century[23] was leading to a systematic process of absorption, a process which lasted exactly one hundred years, from Peter's first initiatives[24] to the triumph of Catherine II.[25]

Both these " Westernizers " of Russia developed there a form of government which, based upon local traditions of autocracy, corresponded to the general trend of " enlightened " absolutism in practically all European countries. Between the German powers, based upon similar political conceptions, which in Prussia were combined with an unusually efficient military organization, and the Russian Empire, proclaimed in 1721, where the reforms of despotic rulers also had predominantly military purposes, Poland, practically disarmed under Russian pressure, kept her traditional constitution[26] based upon the predominance of the Diet and a horror of any *absolutum dominium*. And she remained in that anomalous position until the general revolutionary crisis at the end of the eighteenth century, which was at the same time the end of the so-called " modern " period of European history.

Some historians, especially in the Anglo-Saxon world, go perhaps too far in calling all the changes which occurred in that century simply " revolutionary ". But in addition to the " Great " French Revolution of 1789, at least two real revolutions justify the opinion that it was around this fateful date that what we have called the beginning of the end of the European Age really started. Before briefly considering from that point of view the American Revolution, whose profound significance in this respect is unquestionable, a few words must be said about the Partitions of Poland, which represent the real " diplomatic revolution " of the eighteenth century.[27]

The facts themselves are certainly less neglected in general historiography than are all earlier events of Polish history. But the usual presentation of the causes of the partitions is onesided, strongly influenced by those who want to justify the partitioning powers by casting the responsibilities upon the Poles themselves.[28] And, what chiefly matters here, the consequences of the Partitions, not for Poland alone but for Europe, are almost completely overlooked.

In accordance with the balance of power theory, but contrary to Russia's original intentions, Prussia, and even Austria, which had no interest whatsoever in the annihilation of Poland, received their shares, which were adjusted in difficult negotiations. But there was no compensation whatever for the Western countries corresponding to that aggrandisement of these three powers, and the very structure of the European state system was radically altered. Not only did one of its original members disappear, after an uninterrupted existence throughout the European Age which had included at least three centuries of big power status, but the last free and independent body politic of a whole region of Europe was annihilated.

The importance of that region between Germany and Russia has been discussed in a preceding chapter, where the territorial division of Europe, not into two or three, but into four regions was explained.[29] Of these four regions, the third (counting from the West), East-Central Europe, where only Poland had survived in the modern period, was now completely conquered by powers of the West Central region and by the power which controlled the whole Eastern region, intermediary—as shown above—between the historic European community and Asia. The annexation of the major part of Poland, coming after the conquest of the Ukraine and the Baltic provinces, and not long before the acquisition of Finland, added to old Muscovy so many indisputably European lands that the new Russian Empire as a whole now seemed to be definitely part of the European community, identical with one of its three remaining regions : Eastern Europe. It became at the same time, for the first time in history, the immediate neighbour of a Central Europe completely controlled by German powers, or even of a Western Europe in its larger sense, including all Romance and Germanic nations, which now became inclined to identify the Eastern Slavonic world with Russia, one and indivisible.

The consequences of the Partitions of Poland, considered as a revolution in international policies, explain, therefore, many of the difficulties in the interpretation of the very structure of contemporary Europe which were stressed above on various occasions. But these same partitions appear as an even greater crisis in European history if studied as a revolution in political philosophy and international ethics. They were certainly not the only important violation of moral principles in the relations between the members of the European community. In that same eighteenth century, when moral standards were lower than ever before, an English historian of Poland's partitions, W. F. Reddaway, could compare them, from the moral point of view, with Frederick the Great's rape of Silesia.[30] In the same year 1797, when in a secret additional treaty Poland's disappearance was declared final,[31] another equally old and distinguished member of the European state system, the Republic of Venice, was liquidated. Turkey escaped a partition considered in so many projects of the same years, only because the plans of dismembering Poland instead proved easier to carry into effect. But, after all, Silesia was only a province ; Venice was a once powerful state, but had never been a nation—a distinction which is of the highest importance in the history of Central and Eastern Europe ; Turkey was an intruder in Europe, and it was not actually partitioned.

The case of Poland, therefore, remains unique even in the eighteenth century, when it should have served as a warning that the dissociation of politics and ethics, propagated by Macchiavelli on the eve of modern European history, was destroying, at the end of that period, the very foundations of the European community. The mere fact that, on the contrary, the destruction of Poland was accepted passively and without protest by Europe as a whole as something natural, as much a matter of indifference as if it had happened " on the moon ",[32] less important for the balance of power than the cession of Ochakov by Turkey to Russia[33]—the fact that it hardly moved public opinion even in freedom-loving countries[34]—makes the whole affair a real test of historic Europe's disintegration.

The placing of the Poles under foreign rule was also a test in another issue, both political and moral, which was to have far-reaching implications in the following century. It proved how dangerous it was to violate, on an ever larger scale, the right of the various European nations to full political and cultural freedom in their own states.

The fortunate peoples for whom state and nationality remained identical throughout the whole European age never sufficiently realized the tragedy of others who were victims of foreign conquest. In Western Europe the case of Ireland was exceptional. But in the crucial region which extended between the various Empires of Central and Eastern Europe, imperial expansion had already begun in the Middle Ages to suppress the independence of one nation after another, with the Ottoman conquest as a climax. During the modern period, the various peoples which were gradually united under the Habsburgs lost more and more of their autonomy through the progress of centralization under German leadership. In a similar but more ruthless process under the Russian Tsardom, the main victim was the Ukraine.[35] It is true that the Polish-Lithuanian Commonwealth likewise had failed to solve the Ukrainian problem, and that Polish culture was predominant in the whole federation. But it had not been imposed by force upon any member,[36] while the Partitions brought alien domination to all the peoples of the Commonwealth.[37]

This took place at the very moment when not only had Polish culture reached a new height in its development, but in general all European nationalities, including those which had been enslaved for centuries and even those which had never enjoyed full independence, were becoming more conscious than ever before of their individualities and aspirations, first merely cultural, eventually political also.[38] The resentment of such peoples was therefore particularly strong when, after the Napoleonic wars—which, in spite of their imperialistic character, had raised new hopes among some of these nationalities—the Congress of Vienna not only sanctioned a fourth partition of Poland, but ignored the whole problem of nationalism in general, although in the Balkans a series of wars for independence had just begun.[39]

The principles stressed by the French Revolution certainly contributed to all liberation movements in nineteenth-century Europe, although the Revolution was more concerned with the rights of the individual citizen than with those of national groups. The American Revolution, a successful war for the independence of a new nation, would have been an even greater inspiration for the oppressed European nations, old and new, if it had not been fought in a distant colony on the other side of the Atlantic. But in these colonies it started a movement which, as was pointed out in an earlier chapter, was the clearest possible indication that the free development of European culture in various political units had ceased to be limited to geographical Europe. Here it must be added that, together with the Partitions of Poland, the American Revolution closed the period in which the history of our civilization was decisively influenced by the balance of power in Europe, as it had been influenced in an earlier period by the idea of universalism.

While the Atlantic Age and the making of the Atlantic Community were in their beginning, Europe continued to be in revolution. This statement, made by G. de Reynold in the provocative book stressing the tragic character of Europe's contemporary situation[40] which preceded his study of the formation of Europe, is not in the least paradoxical. There were, first of all, a whole series of individual revolutions in Europe between 1789 and 1917, and the celebration last year of the centenary of 1848 should give us a clearer idea of the real importance even of those revolutions which failed, and of how much they all had in common. But even during the intervals between revolutions, the peaceful, normal character ordinarily attributed to the century between the end of the Napoleonic Wars and the outbreak of the European war in 1914 is somewhat of an illusion. On the contrary, this was a period of tension, typical of the transition from one great age to the next. The old European community seemed to be " restored "[41] by the peacemakers of 1815, but not only was it in a state of " mortal sin "[42] because of the dismemberment of Poland; it was in a state of unrest which becomes apparent to everyone who studies, in addition to the official story of the European Concert, the underground history of all the dissatisfied elements, which include so many nations without states, and social classes which, for the first time, were declared to be in a state of permanent struggle.

In some cases, as in the typically revolutionary year of 1848 and time and again in connection with the troubles caused by the long-delayed liberation of the Balkan nations, the persistent danger of a precarious, critical situation in Europe had to be recognized even by the diplomacy of the privileged big powers. But even in their relations, a twofold threat to the peace and to the very constitution of Europe was apparent, although throughout the century a general war was avoided and practically every conflict was localized.

On the one hand, that permanent threat was represented by Russia, whose advance far into the centre of the continent had already proved so alarming at the time of the Congress of Vienna.[43] The pressure exerted by that power, so much larger than all the other European countries, was hardly reduced even by the temporary setbacks of Russian imperialism which occurred in 1856, 1878, and 1905. That last defeat, in the Far East, made Russia turn even more definitely in the European direction. If this situation did not result in a general conflict earlier, it was because until 1914 Russia continued to have rather good relations with her traditional Prussian ally, who since the disappearance of Poland was her immediate western neighbour. But it was precisely Prussian imperialism which constituted the second threat to Europe's peace. Arising in the very heart of Europe, this imperialism, which had succeeded after three local wars in creating a new, purely national German Empire under Prussia's leadership, with world-wide ambitions, seemed to present a threat greater than that of the other.

In these circumstances first France and then Britain also decided to oppose to Germany's alliance with Austria-Hungary and Italy a Triple Entente which would include Russia, whose co-operation with Germany had to be prevented at any price. It is well known that the division of the European Concert into two armed camps with a prospective aggressor in each of them, far from restoring the balance of power of the preceding period, led to a disastrous European War. But two other facts are equally important. First, the outbreak of that war brought into relief the more obscure causes of Europe's unrest during the transition period of the nineteenth century, particularly the tension arising from the unsolved problem of nationalities. And secondly, it became evident that the history which now entered its crisis was no longer the old European history.

Even among the six big powers which were called European, two were, as a matter of fact, outsiders of the historical European community, and this for different reasons. In the course of the last century, Britain's most important overseas possessions had developed into self-governing dominions; when Britain now entered the war together with these dominions, she did so as part of a world-wide Commonwealth of Nations. During the same nineteenth century, Russia had seemed more European than ever before, but the greatest contribution to civilization which she made in that century, her truly unique literature, " was not culture in the Western classical sense of the world " but just one more proof " that in Russia two streams of world history—East and West—jostle and influence one another ". Nicolas Berdyaev, who rightly considers the nineteenth century " especially illustrative of the Russian idea ", made these statements in order to show that Russia " a complete section of the world . . . is not purely European and is not purely Asiatic ".[44]

Furthermore, as a consequence of nineteenth-century developments, a purely Asiatic country, Japan, and the United States, the American offshoot of European culture, were recognized as two new great powers in the old European sense. In the first of these cases this development proved to be a short-lived illusion, but in the second, a genuine and momentous transformation had occurred which was to merge European and

American history, in spite of the Monroe doctrine. The importance which is given to the nineteenth century in American historiography is, therefore, well justified. But what is not is the belief that the conditions of that century were the normal and typical conditions of Europe and of the world. In European history that period, long called contemporary, amounted to a last attempt to reorganize modern Europe, an attempt which ultimately failed. In universal history it was already the preparation of a new, the Atlantic Age.

CHAPTER X

The Basic Problems of European History

CHAPTER X

The Basic Problems of European History

ONE OF the most comprehensive presentations of modern European history from the Renaissance, including the transition period of the nineteenth century with its extra-European implications—the well-known *Cambridge Modern History*—was planned towards the end of that period by the great English historian Lord Acton. The greatness of his deeply penetrating mind is, however, even more apparent in the plan of another work which he undertook independently—a history of freedom.[1]

The problem of freedom is common to the whole of mankind, without excepting even the primitive societies which have no history in the usual sense. At the end of a life entirely dedicated to the study of the cultural anthropology of such societies, the famous Polish scholar Bronislaw Malinowski prepared a book,[2] published after his untimely death under the suggestive title *Freedom and Civilization*, in which he concludes that freedom and civilization are inseparable, whatever may be the specific character and level of human culture, and on whatever continent that culture may develop. But in the European history of all centuries, freedom in its various aspects is simply *the* problem, the basis of all others and the key to their proper understanding. For that very reason Marxism, which subordinates freedom, along with all other great ideas, to materialistic economic forces, leads to a basically wrong interpretation of human evolution in general and of European history more particularly.[3] Such a doctrine could appear only in the midst of the final crisis of the European Age.

On the contrary, the idea of freedom is closely associated with the earliest foundations of Europe. The very geographical structure of that continent is such as does not favour any forcible unification, and in fact hindered the formation of any Empire which would have dominated all Europe. The struggle for freedom is the most valuable part of the whole tradition of the Mediterranean Age which preceded and prepared the European. Typical of the history of ancient Greece, the problem of freedom is already seen therein in both its main aspects : independence from foreign domination—the goal of the Persian Wars—and the protection of the individual under a free government. Both issues reappear in Roman history, particularly in the time of the Republic, but even then the Romans, so persistent in the defence of their own independence, engaged in conquests without regard for the freedom of other peoples ; and the Roman Empire not only continued in that direction, but sacrificed internal freedom as well to the abuses of imperial authority.

It is true, and quite natural, that the Greeks had already realized the necessity of co-ordinating the principles of freedom and authority. From its earliest origin the European mind was fully aware that freedom must be organized, if it were not to lapse into anarchy. The first experiment in democracy, made by the Athenians in the time of Pericles, was nothing but such an organized freedom within the State ; Athens' failure in creating a freely accepted organization of the relations among the various Hellenic states[4] led to the Peloponnesian War and to defeat. But it was finally the Roman Empire which, in international as well as in national life—to use rather anachronistic expressions—upset the balance between freedom and authority in favour of the latter. This was the heavy price which had to be paid for Roman law and order.

The balance was restored through Christianity. The greatest

contribution which the new religion made to the formation of Europe and to the " discovery of the inner dynamic principles of history "[5] was the restoration, on new and durable because supranational foundations, and the permanent protection of a real freedom based upon the dignity of the human person. But Christianity's main concern was with the freedom of the individual, more particularly of his soul, of the citizen of God's eternal City, while the situation seemed hopeless in that other City, distinguished by St. Augustine,[6] where, in his time of transition, ruthless force prevailed both within the particular states and in their relations.

The idea of freedom was, as a matter of fact, very familiar, though in a rather elementary form, to these ruthless " barbarians " who, after defending their independence against the Empire, created their own political organizations on its ruins. But the interpretation of the primitive conceptions of liberty introduced into European history by the last factor which contributed to Europe's making is no easy task. In that connection, as in so many others, a distinction must be made between the Germanic tribes who, after conquering formerly Roman territories took over the main principles of the Empire, and the Slavonic peoples whose vast majority had only belated and indirect contacts with the imperial tradition.

In making such a distinction we must avoid both the effects of racial interpretation and the exaggerations of wishful thinking. The great Polish historian Joachim Lelewel[7] was not free from such errors when, one hundred years ago, he honestly believed he had found in the pre-historic Slavic communities an early realization of his own generation's ideals of democratic freedom. More recently, the German scholar J. Peisker[8] was equally convinced that because the Slavs had neither liking nor talent for any political organization under a strong authority, they were from the outset fated to succumb to the domination of their Germanic neighbours in the West or "Altaic" invaders from the East. Yet it is certainly true that there always was among the Slavs a special enthusiasm for freedom both external and internal, although their original institutions were neither ideal democracies in the modern sense nor effective guarantees against foreign conquest.

Without, of course, deciding such specific questions here, two preliminary conclusions can be safely emphasized. First, it is obvious that the European idea of freedom can be traced back into Greco-Roman antiquity, being one more link between the Mediterranean Age, when that idea was limited to the European part of the Mediterranean world, and the European Age, when, in one form or another, it became typical of the new community as a whole. Secondly, during the millenary of Europe's making definite progress was made in the growth of that idea, through all the crises of the period, thanks to the Christian inspiration present from the beginning and to the impetus given it by the freedom-loving peoples which one after another joined the European community until it was practically completed in the tenth century.

At that moment in history very promising possibilities seemed to present themselves for a lasting organization of that community, one which would safeguard freedom and at the same time co-ordinate in unity the various elements which had formed historic Europe. If the first millennium of the Christian era had made Europe, the second was characterized by an almost uninterrupted series of attempts at organizing it in such a spirit. This was the main problem of the whole European Age, a two-fold one, as it had been from its Hellenic origin, since it included the constitutional and social issues in the individual states and the even bigger issues of their independence and peaceful relations within a supra-national, universal society. It was at the same time the question of whether or not the Christian principles which were supposed to direct the individual could be applied to national and international life in such a way as to solve at last the old conflict between the claims and necessities of both freedom and order.

It would be impossible to study all these questions in a few pages of a chapter which concludes an investigation into the limits and divisions of European history. The purpose of this chapter is merely to indicate that these limits and divisions in time and space have to be discussed and defined, not only because they are interesting in themselves, but above all because they offer to the historian the indispensable framework for a systematic organization of his material. For if these limits and divisions are well chosen, they will be more than mere forms of presentation; they will serve to make intelligible the very content of the historical process, to emphasize its really decisive aspects, and possibly to reveal its deeper sense. They will likewise contribute to a better understanding of the place of the European Age in universal history.

As a first example of such possibilities, the relationship between the territorial limits of the European community and the problem of freedom may be briefly considered. Whenever in any region of geographical Europe an apparent solution of the basic political issues has been reached by simply suppressing freedom, that region has been placed, at least temporarily, outside historical Europe. This happened, quite obviously, in all cases in which non-European conquerors invading parts of Europe forced upon their populations a despotic foreign domination and an alien culture that would never have been freely accepted. The conquests of the Iberian peninsula by the Arabs, of Russia by the Mongols, of the Balkans by the Osmanlis are the most striking instances of this.

More complex is the case of Moscow, where even after liberation from such an invader, a Christian state of European origin developed a conception of freedom so different from the European as to be practically its negation, with despotism and nihilistic anarchy as alternatives.[9] The ground was, therefore, only too well prepared in that great Empire at Europe's border for what we now call totalitarianism, a system which completely eliminates freedom, and for that very reason would be un-European even if it were not so definitely anti-Christian. The fact that countries in the very heart of Europe, with old, uninterrupted European traditions, could become totalitarian even temporarily was the most serious warning that the European Age was ending and that its great heritage, if it were to survive, must be supported by new forces from outside geographical Europe.

Since it was necessary that these forces should be spiritually European, they could derive only from such an extra-European region as had been an old field of European expansion. As long as that overseas expansion had been merely colonial, it was no real enlargement of historic Europe, because instead of bringing to other shores the great idea of freedom, it meant for the distant dependencies of European powers only exploitation and foreign domination, including a practical enslavement of the natives. Only when European colonies succeeded in creating independent states were new nations able to develop the old European conceptions of free government, to enlarge far beyond any geographical limits the community from which they originated, and to compensate it for possible losses in the old world.

To a certain extent, chiefly in the Latin American republics, native elements which survived and were gradually assimilated shared in that development of freedom.[10] But it is questionable whether Europeans are qualified to propagate their ideas of freedom among peoples of entirely different cultures without destroying these cultures or placing these peoples under rulers of European origin. Only the purely spiritual freedom of Christianity has thus far been propagated in such a way, since the missionary activities, too frequently subject to abuse in the earlier days, were gradually separated from the aims of political and economic colonization or penetration. The amazing progress of " Westernization "—whether Europeanization or Americanization[11]—in the material, technical field is something entirely different, and has nothing to do with the advance of freedom. No extra-European country advanced more rapidly than Japan in technical development on the European or American pattern, but this advance was accompanied by little if any progress in the direction of freedom. A terrible defeat was needed to make that country " safe for democracy ", just as it took a dangerous crisis in the history of the colonial Empires to make Europe admit that the " dependent " peoples of all races had a right to political self-determination in the European sense.

Only if and when the ideas of democratic government and national self-determination, those two equally important achievements of the European trend towards freedom, materialize in all civilized societies will the world, in spite of cultural differences, be really one, federated in an efficient world-organization guaranteeing a lasting peace in freedom, justice, and security. If this noble dream did not become a reality after World War I and is a prospect even more remote after the second, it is because in the European Age, which these two wars concluded, the problem of freedom in its various aspects was not solved even within the limits of the European community. And that, again, was a consequence of the failure of that community, though identified with Christendom, to become organized on truly Christian principles.

This same failure is the cause of the crisis through which Europe and her culture are passing in our times, a cause which is specifically European and bears little relation to any of the regular causes of disintegration, decline and fall which the sociologists try to discover in the parallel developments of all civilizations.[12] An historian who does not believe in any laws regulating human destinies, similar to those governing in-animate nature, who is moreover sceptical of analogies with biological evolution and even of an excess of the comparative method in the interpretation of history,[13] will be inclined to consider the history of each individual civilization as unique in its development. Such an attitude seems particularly justified in the case of our civilization, not because it is ours nor because it is superior to others, but because it is a result of the unique Christian experience and because it came nearer than any other to world-wide expansion.

Strangely enough, it was in the first period of the European Age that Christendom came nearest to a solution of the problem of its political organization. Turning, in that connection, to the divisions of history, we find another example of the close relationship between the apparently formal questions discussed in the present study and the vicissitudes of the basic issue of freedom. The " mediaeval " solution which was an attempt to reconcile unity and diversity was certainly not an unqualified success. Its idealization now would be as great an error as was its indictment during the following periods, in which even less success was experienced in the organization of the European community. Still greater would be the mistake of believing that Europe should or could revert to a " new " Middle Age. But the reasons which doomed the conception of mediaeval univer-salism to failure are in themselves instructive.

The most important of these reasons has already been pointed out ; its relation to the problem of freedom remains to be demonstrated. The political philosophy of the whole period was dominated by the fallacy that Christian universalism must incorporate the idea of a universal Empire, with the imperial authority entrusted to the ruler of an individual nation. Through a misconception of early Christian historiography,[14] it was held that the succession of pagan Empires in the ancient Mediterranean world would be continued until the end of time in the form of a Christianized—hence " Holy "—Roman Empire transferred to the German nation. Not only was this a threat to the freedom of all other nations, but it proved to be the greatest danger to that other truly Christian universal power, the Church.

It would have been another mistake to centralize all power, including the purely political, in the hands of the Papacy, for this, too, would have endangered both freedom and religion. Not even those popes who went furthest in emphasizing the superiority of the spiritual sword over the secular claimed the joint control of both in a papal theocracy. But if it had not been for the imperial interpretation given to the idea of an earthly City reconciled with the City of God,[15] the *Respublica Christiana* could actually have been what its name seemed to imply : a Commonwealth of free and equal Christian states, federated under a freely elected, truly international secular authority. Since no such secular authority was even planned, it was the ecclesiastical authority which, in addition to the rôle which it frequently had to play in protecting human rights against violation by governments, stood as the only possible protector of national freedoms and of the smaller states against the encroachment of the Empire. With one country after another placing itself under the immediate authority of the Holy See, there was a trend towards some kind of a federation of territories outside the Empire under the leadership of the popes in the time of their greatest power.[16] But with the decline of their power, that escape became illusory, and an entirely new solution of what might be called the problem of international European relations was badly needed.

193

Unfortunately such a solution was not reached in the following Renaissance period, which was marked by so great an eagerness to discover the whole world and the individual man. As far as the individual was concerned, his freedom was defended by the humanists against everything which was considered a mediaeval bondage of the mind, but much less against the growing power of state authority. It is true that the development of individualism, national as well as personal, contributed to the independence of every sovereign state from an international authority. But, as a matter of fact, such an authority had practically ceased to exist, since the vanishing universalism of the Middle Ages was not replaced by any better organization of Europe.

Nevertheless certain promising attempts at organizing at least some regions of Europe through federal unions now manifested themselves. The modest mediaeval beginnings of the Swiss Confederation were successfully developed during the Renaissance period ; at its end, the Confederation was, as a matter of fact, independent from the Empire, and united peoples of various languages and denominations.[17] On a much larger scale, federalism was applied in the eastern part of Central Europe. The Jagellonian idea was much more than a dynastic conception and had little in common with Polish nationalism ;[18] it was a programme set forth in union charters and political treaties, which aimed to organize, in a great variety of constitutional forms, the peaceful co-operation of free and equal nations, surrounded by aggressive neighbours. Although the idea was not fully realized in practice, this programme was more successful than the union of the three Scandinavian Kingdoms,[19] which was simultaneously started. Both were typical of the most constructive political conceptions of the Renaissance period.

In general, however, the trend towards secularism which

so clearly distinguishes that second period of the European Age led to rather negative results as far as the organization of the European community was concerned. In that respect, it left to the following period only the balance-of-power idea, which failed to save modern Europe from international anarchy.

Some perspicacious and noble minds of the period were fully aware of the danger. But their far-reaching plans for universal peace remained utopian, while the first rules of international law[20] covered only a limited field of human relations. The integrity and independence of the various members of the European community were no longer seriously threatened by any Empire with pretentions to universality, but instead the imperialism of a few stronger states was a permanent danger to all the others and to European peace.

Moreover the centuries of modern times, in which so much pride has been taken in " progress ", have been, in general, less favourable to the freedom even of the individual citizen than were the despised " Middle Ages ". The liberties which so many famous mediaeval charters guaranteed, at least to important social groups in various countries—the English *Magna Carta* is only one example—were now lost almost everywhere. Even the formerly privileged classes were under the political control of absolute rulers, while the conditions of the peasant population deteriorated into serfdom. Only in exceptional cases, such as the Polish Constitution of May 3, 1791—praised for that reason by Edmund Burke[21]—were reforms accomplished without violent revolution. In general Europe, having abandoned its lofty tradition of organized liberty, was approaching the great revolutionary crisis which began at the end of the eighteenth century.

It is true that there were, in the following century, many examples of constructive, evolutionary reform. In most European countries the freedom of the individual and the rights of the citizen were in process of growth. Only in the two Empires which formally belonged to the European Concert but were built upon foundations different from the common European tradition, Russia and Turkey, was all that was accomplished in that direction definitely too little and too late.[22] Yet everywhere the progress was too slow to meet the new social problems raised by the so-called industrial revolution. And it was hopeless from the start that these reforms should be based upon political or economic expediency, instead of the moral grounds recommended in the papal encyclicals.

Most unfortunate of all was the fact that two other aspects of the crisis were almost entirely neglected. On the one hand, there was the suppression or limitation of the freedom of so many nations whose rights had been violated in the preceding centuries ; now, when their national consciousness was fully developed, such nations had to live under foreign domination.[23] The liberation of the Christian population of the Balkans and the constitutional reforms in the multi-national Habsburg Monarchy were, of course, steps in the right direction, but the former was accompanied by dangerous interventions of rival powers,[24] while the latter were brought about by a " compromise " which resulted in a universal condition of " limited dissatisfaction "[25] and could not possibly solve problems which reached beyond the frontiers of the monarchy.

On the other hand, the problem of international organization which, as is evidenced by the whole course of European history, was an inseparable counterpart of the problem of national freedom received even less attention. The so-called " Concert " of the great European powers was in no sense a permanent organization ; guided only by considerations of power politics and expediency, it succeeded in resolving by appeasement several minor conflicts of interests, but it failed— or, rather, it seemed to be non-existent—when the general tension had reached its climax. Also, the modest results of the two Peace Conferences which shortly before had been held at The Hague[26] had hardly any significance at the decisive moment, since, after all, only lip service had been paid to the high principles of law and justice.

These principles were seriously studied and invoked at the end of the Great European War, but they were not raised in the name of Europe. On the contrary, there even appeared to be a danger that the European balance of power idea would find an enlarged sphere of action. At the end of the Renaissance period, which had experienced the use of that system within the limits of Italy, the balance-of-power idea began to guide international relations in the wider field of European politics.[27] At the end of the European Age it was the even larger—or, rather, the largest possible—field of world politics which began to be directed by that same conception. But again, as in the case of Italy, the narrower field of the earlier period had become the object of outside intervention : non-European forces were fighting on European soil, deciding, together with the diplomacy of a great non-European power, the issues most vital for the future of the continent.

That was a clear indication that historical Europe, during her protracted revolutionary crisis, had lost her last opportunity to work out a satisfactory solution of the problems which had been the main concern of the whole European Age. And, continuing the comparison with Renaissance Italy, it ought to be added that such a failure, in striking contrast with a real progress in so many other domains of life and culture, was the natural consequence of a process of secularization which increasingly dissociated politics from moral values.[28]

It is true that a warning was issued from the authority best qualified to react against such an attitude. The Papacy, which from the middle of the nineteenth century had been rapidly regaining its prestige and at the end of the century had set forth the principles for a solution of the new social problems, raised its voice, in the middle of the European War, in favour of a peace settlement based upon freedom and justice for all.[29] In the same year, 1917, came another warning of an entirely different character. The long series of European revolutions reached a climax in the first totalitarian Revolution of Russian Bolshevism, a movement which propagated, as a solution of both social and political conflicts, a distortion of the idea of freedom that was, as a matter of fact, a suppression of freedom, just as it was a break with the whole European and Christian tradition.

It was at that very moment that a reinterpretation of that tradition, a plea for individual and national freedom, came from America in the Wilsonian peace programme, which rejected the balance-of-power idea, replacing it by the idea of national self-determination under an international organization. That constructive programme was the more difficult to put into practice because it was not limited to Europe. This was only natural, since it was an American plan ; but it was not even limited to the nations with the European and Christian tradition, to the new Atlantic community which was already replacing the European. It was to be worldwide in its scope, universal in a global sense, and in that respect it proved premature. Woodrow Wilson did not even favour the idea of regional groups within the universal League ; he agreed to mentioning such a possibility in the Covenant[30] only to appease American isolationists through a reference to the Monroe doctrine.

Wilson did not succeed in overcoming the American opposition which made the United States reject, together with the Peace Treaty, the League of Nations. But though the new international organization was thus seriously weakened from the outset and though most European powers had little enthusiasm for Wilson's ideas, making him compromise on various points, his initiative was not a failure. On the contrary, it gave what remained of the European community one more opportunity to organize itself in association with a world organization which, in any event, would have chiefly European problems to consider. It therefore was a return to the old European idea of universalism, in an entirely new form, of course, and with the co-operation of some at least of the non-European countries, which on various occasions proved valuable.[31]

The success of the whole experiment, after the withdrawal of the United States, depended on the European countries, which for two decades made great efforts, in Geneva and elsewhere, to organize for a lasting peace of the continent—and, if accomplished, this would have been a decisive step towards world peace. The chances were, after all, much better than they had been in the nineteenth century, because, in spite of many shortcomings in the peace treaties, there was more freedom and justice in Europe than before.[32] Most important in that respect was the liberation of so many nations which had been under foreign rule in the pre-war period. In addition to Eire in North-Western Europe, these were all the nations of the formerly submerged region between Germany and the part of Europe which was lost to the Soviet Union. During the twenty years of independence which were granted to these countries, they all made considerable progress in close connection with Western culture and in co-operation with the Western democracies. It is true that their own democratic development suffered from the fact that they were surrounded by the forces of totalitarianism—after 1933 in control of Germany as well as Russia—by powers radically opposed to the peace settlement after 1918, and to the very existence of the free nations in the intermediary zone between them. But not a single one of these nations turned totalitarian, and, contrary to the misrepresentations of a propaganda of German and Russian inspiration which discredited all their achievements, they were an indispensable element in the reconstruction of Europe.[33]

That reconstruction was violently interrupted, and the last chance of Europe's peaceful organization lost, when, after the first aggressions of Nazism against Austria and Czechoslovakia, the German-Russian co-operation (which can be traced back to the Rapallo Treaty of 1922) resulted in the partition of all East-Central Europe between Nazism and Communism during the years 1939–1941.[34] Since Germany had moreover subjugated most of Western Europe in 1940, and threatened Britain also, the United States felt obliged to interfere, and, together with Britain, decided to assist the Soviet Union when one of the totalitarian powers turned against the other.

This time the war developed into a real world war. Furthermore, four months before Pearl Harbour, America, together with the British Empire, had announced a world-wide peace programme, less specific than Wilson's but in basic agreement with it, as well as with the suggestions made by Pope Pius XII at Christmas in 1939.[35] Had this programme been put into effect, the liberty of all nations, great and small—including, of course, the enslaved countries of Europe—would have been restored and the democratic freedoms of their citizens guaranteed ; a free Europe would have been organized in a free world.

It is hardly necessary to point out that under Soviet pressure the principles of the Atlantic Charter were supplanted by a division of " liberated " Europe and of the world into two spheres, each under the influence of one of the two suprapowers : the United States and Russia. In the Russian " orbit ", a totalitarian Eurasian world, there is no hope for freedom, nor for the future of the large part of Europe forcibly included in it.

America, on the contrary, is assisting the remaining part of Europe, not only in post-war reconstruction, but in forming, at last, a political organization based upon the common Eur-american tradition of Christianity and human freedom, which would permit these European countries and their cultures to survive in the framework of the United Nations, the new universal organization.

After the German defeat in the War of 1914–1918, the German scholar Oswald Spengler predicted the doom of Western—that is, European—civilization ; now, after her even heavier defeat in the last war, another German scholar whose work is less provocative but more thorough, Alfred Weber, has published what he calls a " farewell to European history ".[36] There is more justification for Weber's view than there was for Spengler's prediction of thirty years ago ; yet, understandable though his pessimistic interpretation of the situation is, he carries it too far. His reaction to the breakdown of the balance-of-power system is apparently a willingness to admit that not European only, but that whole history which had its beginning one thousand two hundred years before Christ has come to an end. But actually the end of the European Age—that is, the end of the supremacy of the European community and of a European history which could be studied as a separate unit—does not necessarily mean even that the rôle of historic Europe, of European culture and tradition, has become a thing of the past. Nevertheless the possibility most ably suggested by Arnold Toynbee[37] that Europe, organized and united after an un-precedented catastrophe, might form a third world power, placed between America and Russia and reducing in some inter-mediary function the tension between the two, seems likewise dubious. What appears to be more probable is an increasingly close association of free Europe with America in the Atlantic community of a new age of history. How much of historic

Europe will be free, and permitted to join that community, is a question of the future which the historian is unable to answer, although the study of Europe's historic limits and divisions can contribute to the understanding of the issue.

Entirely outside the historian's competence is another question of the future : whether the rest of the world, all the different cultures which still coexist, and even the whole of Eurasia liberated from its present dictatorship, will ever join in a free universal community of mankind, in the " oecumenical commonwealth " of a " great society " which would inaugurate a truly universal age of history.[38] One thing only is certain : such a result can never be achieved through conquest according to the totalitarian, imperialistic pattern, but only through the advancement of the old European idea of freedom all over the world and through a peaceful conquest of Christian principles, finally introduced into politics. A Christian philosophy of history, supplanting so many wrong interpretations of human destinies, could help us to reach that distant but inspiring goal.

NOTES

Notes

INTRODUCTION

1. Since these articles will not be quoted in the present study, a list of them is given here: (1) " L'histoire de l'Europe orientale, sa division en époques, son milieu géographique et ses problèmes fondamentaux ", *La Pologne au V-me Congrès international des Sciences historiques. Bruxelles 1923* (Varsovie, 1924), 73–94; (2) "Problem średniowiecza (The problem of the Middle Ages) ", *Pamiętnik IV Zjazdu historyków polskich w Poznaniu* (Records of the IVth Congress of Polish historians in Poznań) (Lwów, 1925), 1–7; (3) " W sprawie podziału dziejów powszechnych na okresy (About the division of general history into periods) ", *Przegląd Warszawski*, 5 (1925): 129–148; (4) " Projets d'articles sur les mots *Divisions* et *Moyen Age* ", *Revue de Synthèse historique*, 42 (1936), appendix: 10–22; (5) " Moyen âge et temps modernes ", *Ibid.*, 43 (1927): 69–82; (6) " La division de l'histoire en périodes chronologiques ", *La Pologne au VI-me Congrès international des Sciences historiques. Oslo 1928* (Varsovie, 1930), 1–18; (7) " Qu'est ce que l'Europe Orientale? ", *Bulletin d'Information des Sciences historiques en Europe Orientale*, 6 (1934): 82–93; (8) " Der Begriff der osteuropäischen Geschichte ", *Zeitschrift für osteuropäische Geschichte*, 9 (1934): 1–21; (9) "Europa środkowa (Central Europe)", *Encyklopedia nauk politycznych* (Warszawa, 1937), 2: 127–129; (10) " Kulturgeschichte und Geschichtsphilosophie ", *Wirtschaft und Kultur—Festschrift zum 70. Geburtstag von Alfons Dopsch* (Baden bei Wien, 1928), 684–696; (11) "Europe centrale ou Europe orientale ", *La Voix de Varsovie*, 1 (1940): 5–13; (12) " The Historical Rôle of Central-Eastern Europe ", *The Annals of the American Academy of Political and Social Sciences*, 232 (1944): 9–18; (13) " The Two World Wars—a Comparison ", *Thought*, 21 (1946): 21–44.

2. Arnold J. Toynbee, *A Study of History*, abridged by D. C. Somervell (New York—London, 1947). All quotations in this book are, of course, from the full edition in six volumes (London, 1934–1939; at least three more volumes are to follow), hereafter referred to as Toynbee, *Study*.

3. Gonzague de Reynold, *La Formation de l'Europe* (4 vols., Fribourg en Suisse, n.d., actually published 1944–1945). Each volume has a separate title: (1) *Qu'est ce que l'Europe?*, (2) *Le monde grec et sa pensée*, (3) *L'Hellénisme et le génie européen*, (4) *L'Empire romain*. Hereafter they are all referred to as de Reynold, *Formation*. Two more volumes are in preparation: (5) *Les Romains et les Barbares*, (6) *Le Moyen âge*.

CHAPTER I

1. Hans Helmolt, ed., *Weltgeschichte* (1st ed., 9 vols.—the last containing supplements and bibliographies, Leipzig, 1899–1907). There is an English translation: *The History of the World* (New York, 1902–1907).

2. Toynbee, *Study*, 1: 17 ff.

3. *Ibid.*, 5: 372–376.

4. Most recently by Gilbert J. Garraghan, *A Guide to Historical Method* (New York, 1946), 20.

5. Oswald Spengler, *Der Untergang des Abendlandes* (2 vols., Munich, 1920). The title of the English translation, *The Decline of the West* (by Ch. F. Atkinson, New York, 1926), does not render the full meaning of the German word " Untergang " which involves the idea of complete destruction and disappearance.

6. Lord Macaulay, *Critical, Historical and Miscellaneous Essays* (New York, 1897), 4: 301.

7. de Reynold, *Formation*, 1: 55.

8. Toynbee, *Study*, 1: 132 f.

9. This is the basic conclusion of the French school of human geography, opposed to the determinism of the German "Anthropogeographie " and represented, for instance, by Lucien Febvre (*see* the translation of his *La terre et l'évolution humaine*, under the title *A Geographical Introduction to History*, New York, 1925).

10. Eugène Pittard, *Les races et l'histoire* (Paris, 1924). English translation by V. C. C. Collum (New York, 1926).

11. de Reynold, *Formation*, 3: 35 ff., particularly chapters VII to XIII of that volume, where the " état européen " of Hellenism is studied.

12. Tadeusz Zieliński, *Helenizm a Judaizm* (Hellenism and Judaism, 2 vols., Warszawa, 1927). While many serious objections have been raised to Zieliński's criticism of the Jewish religious tradition, his brilliant interpretation of the religious values preserved in ancient Greece can hardly be questioned; *see* the recent remarks by Stefan Srebrny in *Eos*, 42 (1947): 58–60.

13. One of the first to discuss the rivalry between Sparta and Athens from the point of view of our contemporary experience with totalitarianism v. democracy was the Polish writer Stanislaw Łoś (now professor of Ancient History in the Catholic University of Lublin) in an article published more than twenty years ago in *Przegląd Współczesny* (Contemporary Review); I am unable at present to find the precise reference.

14. In letter XVII of *The Federalist*, ed. Edward M. Earle (Washington, 1939).

15. That was first realized by E. A. Freeman, *History of Federal Government from the Foundation of the Achaian League to the Disruption of the United States* (vol. 1, London—Cambridge, 1863). Only the first part of that work, dealing with ancient Greece, was entirely completed; it is the most important section of the second enlarged edition, prepared by J. B. Bury, under the title *History of Federal Government in Greece and Italy* (London—New York, 1883).

16. de Reynold, *Formation*, 4: 178, 181.

17. *See* my discussion of Renaissance culture in Poland in *The Cambridge History of Poland from the Origins to Sobieski* (Cambridge, now in print), 328.

18. *See* Jacques Maritain's profound interpretation in his study on " Religion and Culture ", *Essays in Order* (ed. Ch. Dawson and T. F. Burns, New York, 1931), 32.

19. de Reynold, *Formation*, 1: 36; " Civilisation européenne est donc synonyme de civilisation chrétienne ".

20. Nobody has better expressed it than Henri Bergson in one of his discussions with Jacques Chevalier, quoted by J. M. Oesterreicher, " Henri Bergson and the Faith ", *Thought*, 22 (1947): 667. *See also* Nicolas Berdyaev, *The Meaning of History* (London, 1936), 111, 123, in the chapter " Christianity and History ".

21. Ferdinant Lot, *Les invasions barbares et le peuplement de l'Europe* (2 vols., Paris, 1937). *See* particularly his introduction (1: 7–8) where he stresses the difference between this book, dealing with a great variety of peoples, and his earlier work limited to *Les invasions germaniques. La pénétration mutuelle du monde barbare et du monde romain* (Paris, 1935).

22. de Reynold tries to show this in the cases of Spain, Portugal, France, Switzerland, Belgium, Holland, England, and to a certain extent even in the Danubian region (*Formation*, 4: 104–154), but we shall see later (chapter II, p. 34) that his arguments are not equally convincing in all these cases.

23. *See* the remarks of Paul Lehmann, " Mittelalter und Küchenlatein ", *Historische Zeitschrift*, 137 (1928): 200 (bibliographical footnote 1)–206.

24. *See* below, Chapter IX, p. 165.

25. There is the same trouble in languages other than English or French, for instance in Polish where " historia nowożytna " (modern) and " nowoczesna " (frequently used instead of " współczesna ", i.e., contemporary) are terms even more difficult to distinguish.

26. Denis de Rougemont and Charlotte T. Muret, *Heart of Europe* (New York, 1941).

CHAPTER II

1. Christopher Dawson, *The Making of Europe* (1st ed., London, 1932; latest ed., New York, 1945).

2. Benedetto Croce, *Teoria e storia della storiographia* (Bari, 1920), 101.

3. Kazimierz Zakrzewski, *Rewolucja Odoakra* (Kraków, 1933, reprinted from the *Rozprawy* of the Polish Academy, Division of Historical and Philosophical Sciences, vol. 68).

4. *See* J. B. Bury's introduction to vol. 4 of the *Cambridge Medieval History*, explaining its title: *The Eastern Roman Empire*.

5. G. Ferrero, *The Ruin of Ancient Civilization and the Triumph of Christianity* (transl. by Lady Whitehead, New York, 1921), 179 ff. M. Rostovtzeff first presented his theory in an address before the International Congress of Historical Sciences held in Brussels in 1923, published in *Musée belge*, 26 (1923; *see* de Reynold's comment, *Formation*, 4: 192 ff.). He developed it in his *Social and Economic History of the Roman Empire* (Oxford, 1926).

6. F. Lot, *La fin du monde antique et le début du moyen âge* (Paris, 1927; English transl. 1931).

7. "Das Zeitalter der Germanen" Oskar Jäger called the Middle Ages in the concluding sentence of the first volume of his *Weltgeschichte* (Bielefeld, 1887), dealing with ancient history.

8. Alfons Dopsch, *Wirtschaftliche und soziale Grundlagen der europäischen Kulturentwicklung aus der Zeit von Cäsar bis auf Karl den Grossen* (2 vols,. 1st ed., Wien, 1918–1920, 2nd ed., Wien, 1923–1924). There is an English translation: *The Economic and Social Foundations of European Civilization* (London, 1927). *See also* his special study " Das Kontinuitätsproblem. Vom Altertum zum Mittelalter ", in Alfons Dopsch, *Beiträge zur Sozial-und Wirtschaftsgeschichte* (Wien, 1938), 253–276. Also Erna Patzelt, " Die Kontinuitätsfrage ", in *Wirtschaft und Kultur—Festschrift zum 70. Geburtstag von A. Dopsch* (Baden bei Wien, 1938), 18–33.

9. Marian H. Serejski, *Idea jedności Karolińskiej* (The idea of Carolingian unity, Warszawa, 1937), is "a study of the mediaeval origin of the European community ".

10. Henri Pirenne, " Un contraste économique: Méfovingiens et Carolingiens ", *Revue belge de philologie et d'histoire, II* (1923).

11. Henri Pirenne, *Mahomet et Charlemagne* (5th ed., Paris—Bruxelles, 1937). There is an English translation: *Mohammed and Charlemagne* (London—New York, 1939). On p. 210 of this book, the author repeated, almost without change, the challenging words which ended his first article published under the same title in *Revue belge de philologie et d'histoire*, I (1922): " Sans Mahomet Charlemagne est inconcevable ". The most important statements quoted below are taken from pp. 123, 126, 143, 163, 211, and from the conclusions, pp. 260–261. A bibliography of reviews and articles discussing Pirenne's thesis has recently been given by Richard N. Frye in footnote 1 to Daniel C. Dennet, " Pirenne and Muhammad ", *Speculum*, XIII (1948), 165 f., where provocative objections against Pirenne's interpretations have been raised; they are, however, not decisive, since they consider almost exclusively his economic arguments.

12. *Ibid.*, pp. 163, 211, and 260, where Pirenne combines the two notions, speaking of " l'unité médiévale du monde antique ".

13. As an illustration to Toynbee's " survey " (*Study*, 1: 57–129) and " classification " (*ibid.*, 1: 129–146) of civilized societies, the following genealogy, using his terminology and based upon his theory of " affiliation " might prove helpful:

208

14. I am not discussing here the problem of a prehistoric culture which appeared in the western basin before the eastern started its historical rôle (*see* de Reynold, *Formation*, 1: 203 f.).

15. The whole problem of that name, including its etymology, is discussed by de Reynold in his chapter on " L'Europe mytologique " (*Formation*, 1: 76–112; *see also* 113–119, on the earliest distinctions between Europe and Asia, or Africa).

16. *See ibid.*, 1: 200–201, on " le caractère préméditerranéen, préeuropéen de l'Asie antérieure ".

17. *Ibid.*, 3: 74–76.

18. The introduction to Book I of Polybius's *Historiae*, quoted by both Toynbee, *Study*, 3: 312 f., and de Reynold, *Formation*, 4: 86 f.

19. Toynbee, *Study*, 1: 53, 134; 4: 2, 3.

20. de Reynold, *Formation*, 3: 52 f., speaks of an "époque impériale" from Alexander the Great to the dissolution of the Roman Empire. He is more convincing when he points out that a new epoch was beginning in the days of Augustus, whom he calls a great, perhaps the first, European (*ibid.* 4: 178).

21. Christopher Dawson, *The Making of Europe*, 5–6; *see*, however, a somewhat different approach of the same author on p. 78.

22. de Reynold, *Formation*, 4: 108–119.

23. Camille Jullian, *Histoire de la Gaule* (8 vols., Paris, 1910–1926); the idea of continuity appears even more clearly in his short, popular outline, *De la Gaule à la France—nos origines historiques* (Paris, 1923).

24. de Reynold, *Formation*, 4: 120–128, 138–154.

25. Pirenne, *Mahomet et Charlemagne*, 2: " L'Empire ne connaît ni Asie, ni Afrique, ni Europe ".

26. This idea which G. Schnürer expressed at the end of his address on the divisions of history, delivered some twenty years ago at the University of Fribourg, is also developed by Nicolas Berdyaev, *The Meaning of History* (London, 1936), 106, 108, and by Jacques Pirenne, *Les grands courants de l'histoire universelle* (Neuchâtel 1945f.), 1: 376.

27. G. Vernadsky, *Ancient Russia* (New Haven, 1944), 48, 77, 101. *See also* Dawson, *The Making of Europe*, 73–74, on the trade routes towards Northern Europe.

28. *See* a brief summary of that discussion in R. W. Seton-Watson, *A History of the Roumanians* (Cambridge, 1934), 9–16.

29. Pirenne, *Mahomet et Charlemagne*, 123.

30. *Ibid.*, 123, 260.

31. *Ibid.*, 143, 261. Even Dawson would say occasionally (p. 286) that the " Carolingian unity " was already the foundation of mediaeval Western civilization. According to L. Halphen, *Charlemagne et l'Empire Carolingien* (Paris, 1947), Europe "was born" between 700 and 900.

32. Dawson, *The Making of Europe*, 196–201; in Part 1 of his Vol. 5, just published (Fribourg, 1949), de Reynold has well explained the rôle of the Celts in the formation of Europe.

33. Toynbee, *Study*, 2: 322–340, 424–433.

NOTES

34. Charles H. Haskins, *The Normans in European History* (Cambridge, Mass., 1915). *See also* Dawson, *The Making of Europe*, 234 ff., on the 'Age of the Vikings ".

35. Toynbee, *Study*, 2: 340–360, 438–443.

36. G. Vernadsky, *Ancient Russia*, 276–278. An article by the Ukrainian philologist Roman Smal-Stocki, giving a new explanation of the origin of that name, will appear in the near future.

37. A. A. Vasiliev, *The Russian Attack on Constantinople in* 860 (Cambridge, Mass., 1946).

38. N. Riasanovsky, " The Norman Theory of the Origin of the Russian State ", *The Russian Review*, 7 (1947): 96–110, defends once more the anti-Normanist theory. *See* the survey of the earlier discussions given by Stuart R. Tomkins, "The Varangians in Russian History ", *Mediaeval and Historiographic Essays in Honor of James Westfal Thompson* (Chicago, 1938), 465–490; and also the new approach of N. K. Chadwick, *The Beginnings of Russian History: an Enquiry into Sources* (Cambridge—New York, 1946).

39. Even Dawson (p. 285) simply says that in the tenth century " the world of the Slavs " was " still pagan and barbarian ", just like the Balts and Finno-Ugrian peoples.

40. F. Dvorník has outlined the leading conceptions of his book on *The Making of Central Europe*, just published (London, 1949), in his articles " The First Wave of the Drang nach Osten ", *The Cambridge Historical Journal*, 7 (1943): 129–145, and " Western and Eastern Traditions in Central Europe ", *Review of Politics*, 9 (1947): 463–481. *See also* his *Les Slaves, Byzance et Rome au IX-e siècle* (Paris, 1926).

41. G. Vernadsky, *Ancient Russia*, 161 ff., gives the latest survey of the Slavic penetration into the Balkans.

42. J. W. Thompson, *Feudal Germany* (Chicago, 1928), 387–528, where, however, the comparison with the American colonization of the West (*see also* pp. xviii–xix) raises serious doubts.

43. Z. Wojciechowski, *Mieszko I and the Rise of the Polish State* (Toruń and Gdynia, 1936).

44. A complete study of that congress, frequently discussed in Polish historiography, is being prepared by St. Kętrzyński. An article by A. Czajkowski will soon appear in *Speculum*. At present, *see* M. Z. Jedlicki, "La création du premier archevêché polonais à Gniezno", *Revue historique de droit français et étranger* (1943), 643–695.

45. *See* Dawson, *The Making of Europe*, 281–282, where the picture mentioned in the text is reproduced and explained.

46. On the 950th anniversary of the death of St. Adalbert, a collective work *Św. Wojciech 997–1947* was published by the Primate of Poland (Gniezno, 1947); one of the contributions, by Z. Wojciechowski, appeared in English in *The Western Review* (special number for abroad, July–Aug. 1947), 17–28.

47. Pirenne, *Mahomet et Charlemagne*, 143.

48. *Ibid.*, 260.

49. G. Schlumberger, *L'Epopée byzantine* (3 vols., Paris, 1896–1905).

NOTES

CHAPTER III

1. Eric Fischer, *The Passing of the European Age—a Study of the Transfer of Western Civilization and Its Renewal on Other Continents* (Cambridge, Mass., 1943), p. vi. A new edition of this book appeared in 1948.

2. *Ibid.*, 201.

3. *Ibid.*, 177.

4. Toynbee, *Study*, 1: 51.

5. The conversion of the Lithuanians has been recently discussed in English by Thomas G. Chase, *The Story of Lithuania* (New York, 1946), 14, 23–25, 31–32, 40, and Constantine R. Jurgela, *History of the Lithuanian Nation* (New York, 1948), 73–74, 83–87, 127–128. The most detailed study of the problem remains, however, the Polish monograph by Mons. Jan Fijałek in the collective work *Polska i Litwa w dziejowym stosunku* (Poland and Lithuania in their historical relations, Warszawa, 1914), 37–333, preceded by a shorter essay of W. Abraham, 1–32.

6. A revised edition of Donald Attwater's *The Christian Churches of the East, II, Churches separated from Rome* (Milwaukee, 1948) has just been published.

7. On the Ottonian Renaissance, with its climax precisely about 1000, *see* P. E. Schramm, *Kaiser, Rom und Renovatio* (Leipzig, 1929). A well-known work is Charles H. Haskins, *The Renaissance of the Twelfth Century* (Cambridge, Mass., 1927).

8. The most complete study of these plans of international—practically European—organization is Jacob Ter Meulen, *Der Gedanke der internationalen Organisation in seiner Entwicklung*, 3 vols. (Haag, 1917–1940).

9. Carlton J. H. Hayes, *The Historical Evolution of Modern Nationalism* (New York, 1931), 288–302, *see also* his *Essays on Nationalism* (New York, 1926), 52 f.

10. This is particularly emphasized by the Norwegian scholar Halvdan Koht (*see* his articles " Nationalism ", *Bulletin of the Polish Institute*, 3 (1945): 614–620, and " The Dawn of Nationalism in Europe ", *American Historical Review*, 52 (1947): 265–280), but appears also in Hans Kohn, *The Idea of Nationalism* (New York, 1944), who even starts with " Israel and Hellas ".

11. A. S. Atiya, *The Crusade in the Later Middle Ages* (London, 1938).

12. Chapter I, p. 8.

13. The very term, made familiar by Arnold Toynbee, *The Industrial Revolution of the Eighteenth Century in England* (London, 1884), and now universally accepted, is, therefore, open to criticism.

14. Toynbee, *Study*, 3: 158; *see also* his introductory remarks (1: 2–5) on " The industrialization of historical thought ".

15. *See* the famous passage in *Les deux sources de la morale et de la religion* (7th ed., Paris, 1932), 334–335.

16. Sidney B. Fay, " The Idea of Progress ", *American Historical Review*, 52 (1947): 244.

17. Carlton J. H. Hayes, *A Generation of Materialism 1871–1900* (New York, 1941).

18. Gustav Schnürer, *Kirche und Kultur im Mittelalter* (3 vols., Paderborn, 1927–1930).

19. J. J. Walsh, *The Thirteenth—Greatest of Centuries* (New York, 1907).

20. L. Pastor, *History of the Popes,* I (transl. London, 1891): 13.

21. Toynbee, " Churches and Civilizations ", *The Yale Review,* 37 (1947): 1–8.

22. Ross J. S. Hoffman, *The Great Republic* (New York, 1942), 17.

23. Elizabeth V. Souleyman, *The Vision of World Peace in Seventeenth- and Eighteenth-Century France* (New York, 1941).

24. Toynbee, *Study,* 4: 3.

25. What Toynbee says about Napoleon's Empire as a " universal state " (*Study,* 5: 619–642; *see also* 6: 327, on the chart) which created a *pax oecumenica* in Western society is hardly convincing.

26. *See* the chapter " Relations with France to 1536 ", in R. B. Merriman, *Suleiman the Magnificent* (Cambridge, Mass., 1944), 126–144.

27. *See* the analysis of the eight " big powers " by the Swedish geographer Rudolf Kjellén, *Die Grossmächte der Gegenwart* (Leipzig, 1914) whose interpretation so strongly influenced the German school of " geopolitics ", including the famous Haushofer.

28. The continuity of the revolutionary ideology from 1789 to the present, emphasized by G. de Reynold, *L'Europe tragique* (Paris, 1935; *see* below, chapter IX), has been recently shown by Geoffrey Bruun, " The Heritage of Jacobinism ", *Fordham University Studies* (Burke Society Series, No. 2, New York, 1946), 25–35, particularly on p. 24. *See also* Sigmund Neumann, *Permanent Revolution* (New York, 1942).

29. *U.S. Foreign Policy: Shield of the Republic* (Boston, 1943), 114–136; *U.S. War Aims* (Boston, 1944), 63–88.

30. *The Great Republic* (New York, 1942) 162, where the Atlantic is well described as " what is now the inner sea of Christendom "; *Durable Peace* (New York, 1944), 106–116; " Europe and the Atlantic Community ", *Thought,* 20 (1945), 25.

31. *See* A. Paul Levack, "The Atlantic Community as a Historical Concept", *Bulletin of the Polish Institute,* 3 (1945): 601–609, especially his concluding remarks about the interpretation of the Age of Discovery.

32. This limitation is the basic mistake in Lippman's definition of the Atlantic Community (*U.S. Foreign Policy,* 129–134), which ignores the part of all the Central European nations in the settlement of the New World.

33. Moorhouse V. Millar, "American Federalism and European Peace", *Thought,* 18 (1943); *see* particularly 625–635.

34. *The Passing of the European Age,* 177, 200, 201.

35. Carlton J. H. Hayes, " The American Frontier—Frontier of What? ", *American Historical Review,* 51 (1946): 199–216; *see* particularly p. 214.

36. *See* the summary of his address before the Princeton University Bicentennial Conference on *The University and Its World Responsibilities* (Princeton, 1946), 9–10.

NOTES

37. Best evidenced in the nineteen Bulletins on *Progress of Medieval and Renaissance Studies in the U.S. and Canada,* ed. J. W. Willard and S. Harrison Thomson (Boulder, 1924–1947).

38. *The Passing of the European Age,* Chapter IV, 75–94.

39. *See* the latest summary of Toynbee's ideas in *Civilization on Trial* (New York, 1948), 158.

40. Wendell L. Willkie, *One World* (1st ed., New York, 1943).

41. This is the basic mistake of Julian Huxley, *UNESCO—Its Purpose and Its Philosophy* (Paris, 1946); *see* particularly pp. 6 ff.

42. W. B. Ziff, *Two Worlds* (New York, 1946); N. S. Timasheff, *Three Worlds—Liberal, Communist, and Fascist Society* (New York, 1946).

CHAPTER IV

1. Well shown by René Ristelhuber, *La double aventure de Fridtjof Nansen* (Montréal, 1944).

2. *See* the source material in R. Haklyut, *Voyages,* I–II (Everyman's Library Ed., London, 1932).

3. G. Vernadsky, *Medieval Russian Laws* (New York, 1947), 17–19, recently gave a short survey of the importance of Novgorod. *See also* his bibliography (p. 99), the chapter " City–State " in his latest book *Kievan Russia* (New Haven, 1948), 196–201, and the chapter (III) " Novgorod, gateway to Europe and the Urals " in Robert J. Kerner, *The Urge to the Sea* (Berkeley, 1942), 25–34.

4. Toynbee, *Study,* 4: 88; 6: 191, is entirely right in stressing the basic importance of that date in Russian history, but goes too far in interpreting it as the beginning of a " universal state " with a *pax oecumenica* lasting until 1881.

5. Halvdan Koht and Sigmund Skard, *The Voice of Norway* (New York, 1944), 73.

6. Out of the many contributions of Polish historiography to that problem, one appeared also in German: W. Sobieski, *Der Kampf um die Ostsee* (Leipzig, 1933). An English translation of W. Konopczyński's new book *Kwestia bałtycka do XX w.* (The Baltic Question to the XXth Century, Gdańsk, 1947) is in preparation; he also included the recent results of Scandinavian historiography.

7. *See* Charles E. Hill, *The Danish Sound Dues and the Command of the Baltic* (Durham, N.C., 1926).

8. Rightly emphasized in the numerous publications of Alfred Bilmanis; *see,* for instance, his book *The Baltic States and the Baltic Sea* (Washington, 1943), particularly p. 46, and also his *Baltic Essays* (Washington, 1945), particularly pp. 206–211.

9. Dawson, *The Making of Europe,* 252; Koht and Skard, *The Voice of Norway,* 2.

10. Toynbee, *Study,* 2: 340–360.

11. *Ibid.,* 2: 322–340. *See* above, Chapter II, p. 38.

12. *See* the rich material in *The Journal of the American-Irish Historical Society,* 1898 ff.

13. Count R. Coudenhove-Calergi, the founder of the Pan-European movement, who originally excluded Britain from the projected European Union, has now changed his opinion in that matter.

14. A. Zimmern, *The Third British Empire* (3rd ed., London, 1934); *see also* the recent remarks of Alfred Cobban, *National Selfdetermination* (Chicago, 1948), 80 ff.

15. J. Huizinga, "How Holland Became a Nation", *Lectures on Holland for American Students*, 1924, 1–18; *see* on his position in historiography the recent remarks of B. H. Sticher van Bath in *Speculum*, 23 (1948): 247–248. On H. Pirenne and his *Histoire de la Belgique see* the brief, but highly laudatory, remarks of J. P. Gooch, *History and Historians in the Nineteenth Century* (New York, 1928), 447.

16. Louis Bréhier, *L'Eglise et l'Orient au Moyen Age—Les Croisades* (5th ed., Paris, 1928) has a special appendix, pp. 375–388, on the outstanding French participation in the Crusades.

17. Louis Réau, *L'Europe française au siècle des Lumières* (Paris, 1938).

18. de Reynold, *Portugal* (Paris, 1936). He has even called the whole Iberian peninsula " une Eurafrique " (*Formation*, 1: 198).

19. R. B. Merriman, *The Rise of the Spanish Empire* (New York, 1918–34), 1: 4–6.

20. Dawson, *The Making of Europe*, 167–168.

21. Salvador de Madariaga, *Spain* (New York, 1943), 22, says that the Iberian peninsula has " an oriental value of its own ".

22. de Reynold, *Formation*, 1: 142.

23. The great Polish poet, Juliusz Słowacki, translated his *El Principe constante*, a striking proof of the truly European appeal of that story of a Portuguese prince of the fifteenth century.

24. André Siegfried, *The Mediterranean* (New York, 1948).

25. Well explained by Jacques Pirenne, *Les grands courants*, I: 179, 219, 220.

26. Charles Diehl, *L'Afrique byzantine* (Paris, 1895).

27. R. Grousset, *Histoire des Croisades* (3 vols., Paris, 1934–1936); A. S. Atiya, *The Crusade in the Later Middle Ages* (London, 1938), 345–378.

28. R. B. Merriman, *Suleiman the Magnificent* (Cambridge, Mass., 1944), 227–229.

29. The growing interest of American historiography in the history of Liberia appeared in two recent books: Charles H. Huberich, *The Political and Legislative History of Liberia* (2 vols., New York, 1947), and Charles M. Wilson, *Liberia* (New York, 1947); both discussed in the *American Historical Review*, 53 (1948): 797–799.

30. Tibor Eckhardt, "The War of the Twentieth Century", *Thought*, 22 (1947): 427. The question whether the Mediterranean is now an "American life-line " has recently been raised by William Reitzel, *The Mediterranean: Its Role in American Foreign Policy* (New York, 1948).

31. R. B. Merriman, *Suleiman the Magnificent*, 285.

32. H. Kretschmayr, *Geschichte von Venedig*, 3 (Stuttgart, 1934): 315–341.

33. *Ibid.*, 3: 61–62. On the Lusignan's *see* N. Iorga, *Philippe de Mézières*

et la Croisade au XIV-e siècle (Paris, 1896); on Britain and Cyprus, Dwight E. Lee, *Great Britain and the Cyprus Convention Policy of* 1878 (Cambridge, Mass., 1934).

34. Cyril E. Black, " The Turkish Straits and the Great Powers ", *Foreign Policy Reports* (Oct. 1, 1947), has an excellent bibliography of the problem in its usual interpretation.

35. de Reynold, *Formation*, 1: 199–201; 3: 75.

36. For instance in his brilliant synthesis *Byzance—Grandeur et décadence* (Paris, 1919); *see also Histoire Générale, Histoire du Moyen Age*, 3 (Paris, 1936): 499.

37. H. Grégoire, " The Historical Element in Western and Eastern Epics ", *Byzantion*, 16 (1944), 527 ff. *See also* his book on *Digenis Akritas* (New York, 1942) published in modern Greek.

38. On the consequences of the battle of Mantzikiert, in 1071, *see* Ch. Diehl, *Le Monde oriental de* 395 *à* 1081 (*Hist. gén., Hist. du Moyen Age*, vol. 3 (Paris, 1936), 562).

39. A. Gardner, *The Lascarids of Nicaea; the Story of an Empire in Exile* (London, 1912).

40. A. A. Vasiliev, " The Empire of Trebizond in History and Literature ", *Byzantion*, 15 (1940–1941): 316–377.

41. This important date, completely ascertained—*see* f.i. H. A. Gibbons, *The Foundations of the Ottoman Empire* 1300–1402 (Oxford, 1916, p. 101)—continues to be wrongly given in many text-books.

42. About the date of its final loss, *see* P. Charanis, " The Strife among the Palaeologi and the Ottoman Turks, 1370–1402 ", *Byzantion*, 16 (1944): 297.

43. O. Halecki, *The Crusade of Varna* (New York, 1943), 61–64.

44. *See*, for instance, his *Geschichte des Osmanischen Reiches* (Gotha, 1909), 2: 197.

45. Toynbee, *Study*, 2: 77, 177 f., 222.

46. A. H. Lybyer, *The Government of the Ottoman Empire in the Time of Suleiman the Magnificent* (Cambridge, Mass., 1913); *see* the enthusiastic conclusion on p. 198. Toynbee's interpretation and Merriman's chapter on Suleiman's government (*op. cit.*, 145–174, *see also* 308) are mainly based upon that monograph.

47. Toynbee, *Study*, 3: 22–50.

48. *See* the paper read at the International Congress of Historical Sciences, Warsaw, 1933, by Köprülü Zade Fouad Bey (*Résumés*, 1: 297–302).

49. A. S. Atiya, *The Crusade in the Later Middle Ages*, 476–477.

50. H. Pirenne, *A History of Europe from the Invasions to the Sixteenth Century* (New York, 1939), 496–498; *see also* Jacques Pirenne, *Les grands courants*, 2: 260 ff., 310.

51. Stephen P. Lordas, *The Exchange of Minorities—Bulgaria, Greece, Turkey* (New York, 1932).

52. H. W. V. Temperley (ed.), *A History of the Peace Conference of Paris*, 6 (London, 1924): 23–39; *see also* J. T. Shotwell and F. Déak, *Turkey and the Straits* (New York, 1940), 105–113.

NOTES

53. Robert J. Kerner and Harry N. Howard, *The Balkan Conferences and the Balkan Entente* 1930–1935 (Berkeley, 1936), 49, 62, 120–123, 128.

54. Max Silberschmidt, *Das orientalische Problem zur Zeit der Entstehung des Türkischen Reiches nach venezianischen Quellen* (Leipzig, 1923).

55. Marian Małowist, *Kaffa—Kolonia genueńska na Krymie a problem wschodni w latach* 1453–1475 (Caffa—a Genuese colony in the Crimea and the Eastern question, Warszawa, 1947).

56. W. E. D. Allen, *A History of the Georgian People* (London, 1932).

57. An *Armenian Quarterly* has recently (1946) been founded in New York by the Armenian American Cultural Association, and an *Armenian Review* (also quarterly)—in 1948, in Boston, Mass.

58. H. W. V. Temperley (ed.), *A History of the Peace Conference of Paris*, 6: 83–88.

CHAPTER V

1. Reproduced in G. Vernadsky, *Ancient Russia*, between pp. 88 and 89.

2. de Reynold, *Formation*, 1: 135–138.

3. *See*, for instance, the interpretation of the Italian Alessandro Guagnini from Verona who published in 1578, in Cracow, his *Sarmatiae Europeae Descriptio*.

4. *See* above, Chapter IV, p. 67.

5. Robert J. Kerner, *The Urge to the Sea*, 68–79; *see also* his recent article " The Russian Eastward Movement: Some Observations on its Historical Significance ", *Pacific Historical Review*, 17 (1948): 135–148.

6. Roger Dow, " Prostor: a Geopolitical Study of Russia and the United States ", *The Russian Review*, 1 (1941): 6 f.

7. Kerner, *The Urge*, 67; A. Lobanov-Rostovsky, *Russia and Asia* (New York, 1933).

8. G. Vernadsky, *Ancient Russia*, 64.

9. *See*, for instance, Elisée Reclus, *Nouvelle géographie universelle*, 5 (Paris, 1885): 279.

10. *See* above, Chapter IV, p. 80.

11. Thomas G. Masaryk, *Russland und Europa*, 2 vols. (Berlin, 1913); the English translation (New York, 1919) has the less expressive title *The Spirit of Russia*. Recently Nicolas Berdyaev, *The Russian Idea* (New York, 1948), 44, has called that same problem " the fundamental Russian theme ". This chapter was already written when I found in G. Vernadsky's new book *Kievan Russia* (New Haven, 1948) an introductory chapter on " Kievan Russia's Place in History " (1–18) where the question " Is Russia Europe? " and " the notion of East European history " are briefly discussed. Without entering here into minor controversial issues, I should like to quote the statement " that if Russia is Europe, she is only partly so, and that more often than not her historical ways have been different from those of other European powers " (p. 3).

12. Paul Milyukov, *Outlines of Russian Culture* (ed. M. Karpovich, 3 vols., Philadelphia, 1942), is an abridged translation of his standard work (5th ed., in 4 vols., St. Petersburg, 1903–1905) where the third part is a discussion of the issue: nationalism versus " Evropeizm ".

13. Jan Kucharzewski, *The Origins of Modern Russia* (New York, 1948), 240–244; *see* in the full Polish text of his work the chapter on " the legend of the rotten west " (*Od Bialego caratu do czerwonego*, I, Warszawa, 1926, ch. 8), particularly pp. 281–288.

14. " Russland ist was Europa war ", as Masaryk put it. Recently quoted and discussed in the introduction to Valentin Gitterman, *Geschichte Russlands* (Zürich, 1944), I: 12. Cf. *The Spirit of Russia*, 1: 6.

15. Boris Ishboldin, " The Eurasian Movement ", *The Russian Review*, 5 (1946): 64–73; *see* particularly the conclusions, and the earlier study, under the same title, by D. S. Mirsky, *Slavonic Review*, 5 (1927): 311–319.

16. *See* the summary of his lecture on " The Nationalism of Russian Slavophils ", *Bulletin of the Polish Institute*, 1 (1943): 554–556.

17. *See* the latest discussion of his famous " Philosophical letter " by Hans Kohn, " The Permanent Mission ", *Review of Politics*, 10 (1948): 274–276.

18. Many other revealing statements which illustrate the Russian interpretation of Panslavism are quoted and discussed by W. Lednicki, "Panslavism", in Feliks Gross (ed.), *European Ideologies* (New York, 1948), Chapter XXII, 808–912.

19. *See* the significant passage quoted by Hans Kohn, *The Idea of Nationalism* (New York, 1944), 570.

20. L. v. Ranke, *Geschichte der romanischen und germanischen Völker von 1494 bis 1514* (Berlin, 1825); *see* pp. 1 and 3 of the English translation by Ashworth (London, 1889).

21. Particularly in the works of Th. Schiemann, Otto Hoetzsch and Hans Uebersberger, who occupied the chair of East European history in the University of Berlin and edited the *Zeitschrift für Osteuropäische Geschichte*.

22. *See*, for instance, de Reynold, *Formation*, 1: 54.

23. *Ibid*, 3: 385–408, the chapter on " L'Hellénisme de la Grèce moderne".

24. S. H. Cross, " The Results of the Conversion of the Slavs from Byzantium ", *Annuaire de l'Institut de Philologie et d'Histoire Orientales et Slaves*, 7 (1939–1944): 71–82.

25. *See* above, Chapter II, p. 38.

26. F. Dvorník, "The Kiev State and Its Relations with Western Europe", *Transactions of the Royal Historical Society*, 29 (1947): 27–46.

27. Bernard Leib, *Rome, Kiev et Byzance à la fin du XI-e siècle* (Paris, 1924). Joseph B. Koncevičius, *Russia's Attitude towards Union with Rome* (Washington, 1927), 55, goes even further and tries to prove that Russia was not definitely separated from the Roman Church before the end of the twelfth or the beginning of the thirteenth century.

28. A. M. Ammann, *Kirchenpolitische Wandlungen im Ostbaltikum* (*Orientalia Christiana Analecta*, 105, Roma, 1936), 53, 80–82, 146–152, 207–208, 228–229, etc.

29. G. Vernadsky, *Ancient Russia*, 326, even says that " the first Slavic pioneers must have appeared there (in the Rostov-Suzdal region) in the eighth if not in the seventh century ".

30. Robert J. Kerner, *The Urge to the Sea*, 35 ff.

31. N. de Baumgarten, " Généalogies et mariages occidentaux des Rurikides russes du X-e au XII-e siècle ", *Orientalia Christiana*, IX, 1 (Roma, 1927).

32. The decisive importance of that year is particularly stressed in Ukrainian historiography; *see*, for instance, M. Hrushevsky, *A History of Ukraine* (New Haven, 1940), 94, and also the recent interpretation by G. Vernadsky, *Kievan Russia* (New Haven, 1948), 220–221.

33. Toynbee, *Study*, 2: 154. That example would offer an excellent illustration of what he calls (2: 31 ff.) " the stimulus of hard countries ".

34. L. v. Ranke, *op. cit.*; H. Pirenne, *A History of Europe from the Invasions to the Sixteenth Century* (New York, 1939), 466.

35. *Loc. cit.*, 81. A. Toynbee, " Russia's Byzantine Heritage ", *Civilization on Trial* (New York, 1948), goes too far in stressing the Byzantine roots of Russia's contemporary totalitarianism.

36. G. Vernadsky, *Political and Diplomatic History of Russia* (Boston, 1936), 455 (in the list of Grand-Dukes of Moscow).

37. S. Tomashivsky, " Predtecha Isidora " (A precursor of Isidor), *Analecta Ordinis S. Basilii Magni*, 2 (1927).

38. N. Chubaty, " Zachidna Ukraina i Rim v XIII v." (The Western Ukraine and Rome in the Thirteenth Century), *Zapysky Tov. im. Shevchenka*, 123–124 (1917).

39. H. Paszkiewicz, *Polityka ruska Kazimierza W.* (The Ruthenian policy of Casimir the Great, Warszawa, 1925), and *Jagiellonowie a Moskwa*, I (The Jagellonians and Moscow, Warszawa, 1933).

40. I studied the history of the Polish–Lithuanian Federation in my book *Unia Jagiellońska* (The Jagellonian Union, 2 vols., Kraków, 1919–1920); *see also* my articles " L'évolution historique de l'Union polono-lithuanienne ", *Le Monde Slave*, 3 (1926): 279–293, and " L'Union de Lublin ", *Revue historique*, 133 (1920): 258–263. Here again it is interesting to quote from Vernadsky's new book (*see* above, note 11); in discussing the Polish-Lithuanian Federation, which included the Ukrainian and Byelorussian lands, and had close relations with Bohemia, Hungary, and Rumania, he says: " It is the Polish sphere of cultural influence, which may be called the nucleus of eastern Europe in the later Middle Ages and early modern period " (p. 11).

41. A. E. Presniakov, *Obrazovanye Veliko-Russkago Gosudarstva* (The Formation of the Great-Russian State, Petrograd, 1918).

42. G. Vernadsky, *Political and Diplomatic History of Russia* (Boston, 1936), 140, considers, however, already the creation of the Khanate of Kasimov, around 1452, the turning point in Moscow's relations with the Tartars.

43. That year, given in the text of the treaty, is exact, contrary to L. Kolankowski's opinion, admitted by Vernadsky, that it ought to be corrected to 1448; *see* my remarks in *Kwartalnik historyczny* (Historical Quarterly), 51 (1927).

44. P. Pierling, *La Russie et le Saint Siège*, I (Paris, 1896), has a chapter which is entitled "La Renaissance à Moscou", but quite recently Elie

Denissoff, *Maxime le Grec et l'Occident* (Louvain, 1943), 379, remarked that this Renaissance " n'était encore qu'un léger zéphyr incapable de faire fondre la couche de glace qui recouvrait la terre moscovite livrée sans défense pendant les deux siècles de domination tartare à l'emprise de l'Asie ".

45. *See* my study " Les trois Romes " submitted to the VIIth International Congress of Byzantine Studies, Brussels, 1948, and published in *Le Flambeau*, 31 (1948): 277–290.

46. *See* his article " On Some Parallel Trends in Russian and Turkish History ", *Transactions of the Connecticut Academy of Arts and Sciences*, 36 (1945): 25–36, and also *Political and Diplomatic History of Russia*, 170–174.

47. His famous correspondence with Prince A. A. Kurbsky, recently discussed by Harold Lamb, *The March of Muscovy* (Garden City, 1948), 150–152, is published in *Sochinenya kn. Kurbskago* (Works of Prince K., I, St. Petersburg, 1914).

48. Hans Kohn, *The Idea of Nationalism* (New York, 1944), 563.

49. Toynbee, *Study*, 2: 176.

50. *Loc. cit.*, 82.

51. G. P. Fedotov, *The Russian Religious Mind* (Cambridge, Mass., 1946).

52. Clarence A. Manning, *The Story of the Ukraine* (New York, 1947), 106–120, in the chapter " The Spread of Kievan Culture in Moscow ".

53. This appears clearly from R. W. Seton-Watson's recent survey of " Main Currents in Russian Foreign Policy ", *Transactions of the Royal Historical Society*, 29 (1947): 167–186, just because he limits himself almost exclusively to these last two centuries.

54. Paul Hazard, *La crise de la conscience européenne*, 1680–1715 (2 vols., Paris, 1935).

55. Emile A. Haumant, *La culture française en Russie*, 1700–1900 (Paris, 1910).

56. J. S. Curtis, *Church and State in Russia* (New York, 1940).

57. *See*, for instance, Harold Nicolson, *The Congress of Vienna* (New York, 1946), 120.

58. Toynbee, *Study*, 3: 200–202; 6: 343 n. 1.

59. *See* the manifesto of the Supreme Council of Soviets, of Nov. 13, 1918, published by J. W. Wheeler-Bennett, *The Forgotten Peace—Brest-Litovsk, March*, 1918 (New York, 1939), Appendix X.

60. *Nazi-Soviet Relations* 1939–1941 (Washington, Dep. of State, 1948), 78, 107.

61. That expression is used by Walter Lippman, *U.S. War Aims* (Boston, 1944), 89. *The Strange Alliance* is the title of General John Russel Deane's revealing book (New York, 1947) on " the story of our efforts at wartime co-operation with Russia ".

62. On the importance of Petsamo, *see* E. v. Kuehnelt-Leddihn, " The Petsamo Region ", *The Geographical Review*, 34 (1944), 405–417; on the historic rôle of Cetatea Alba (Akkerman), *see* N. Iorga, *Studii istorice asupra Chiliei si Cetatii Albe* (Bucuresci, 1900).

NOTES

CHAPTER VI

1. F. S. C. Northrop, *The Meeting of East and West* (New York, 1946).
2. J. Bidlo, " Ce qu'est l'histoire de l'Orient européen ", *Bulletin d'Information des Sciences historiques en Europe orientale* ", 6 (1934): 11–73.
3. Marceli Handelsman " Quelques remarques sur la définition de l'histoire de l'Europe orientale ", *ibidem*, 74–81; J. Bidlo, " Remarques à la défense de ma conception de l'histoire de l'Europe orientale ", *ibidem*, 95–119; J. Pfitzner, " Die Geschichte Osteuropas und die Geschichte des Slaventums als Forschungsproblem ", *Historische Zeitschrift*, 150 (1934): 21–84; J. Bidlo, " L'Europe orientale et le domaine de son histoire ", *Le Monde Slave*, 12 (1935), 1–20; *see also* my articles quoted in the first footnote of this book under 7 and 8.
4. Toynbee, *Study*, 1: 132 f.
5. de Reynold, *Formation*, 1: 55; *see* above, Chapter I, p. 11.
6. J. Bidlo, *Dějiny Slovanstva* (History of the Slavs, Praha, 1926).
7. M. Lhéritier, *L'Europe orientale à l'époque contemporaine* (Paris, 1938).
8. H. Seton Watson, *Eastern Europe between the Two Wars* (Oxford, 1945).
9. Rudolf Schlesinger, *Federalism in Central and Eastern Europe* (New York, 1945), 386, has to admit it in spite of his pro-Soviet attitude. On the Russification under the Soviet régime, *see also* W. Baczkowski, *Towards an Understanding of Russia* (Jerusalem, 1947), 189–199.
10. All these distinctions, and particularly the last one, appear most clearly in St. Smolka, *Les Ruthènes et les problèmes religieux du monde russien* (Rome, 1916). *See also* above, Chapter V, pp. 91–94.
11. F. Dvornik, *Les Slaves, Byzance et Rome au IX-e siècle* (Paris, 1926); *see also* Th. Haluščynsky, *Acta Innocentii III* (Roma, 1945), 47–53.
12. *See* above, Chapter IV, pp. 68–69.
13. A. Kleinklausz, *Charlemagne* (Paris, 1934), 169–173, with map.
14. About these discussions *see*, for instance, J. W. Thompson, *Feudal Germany* (Chicago, 1928), 267.
15. *See* A. Brackmann, " Die Ostpolitik Otto's des Grossen ", *Historische Zeitschrift*, 134 (1926): 242–256.
16. de Reynold: *Formation*, 4: 148.
17. James Bryce, *The Holy Roman Empire* (New York, 1930), 184–185. *See also* 186 (on Sweden and Norway) and Note B (533–534).
18. W. Norden, *Das Papsttum und Byzanz* (Berlin, 1903), 89–101, 127–132; A. A. Vasiliev, *History of the Byzantine Empire* (Madison, 1928–1929); Charles Diehl, in *Histoire du Moyen Age*, 3 (Paris, 1936): 469, and 9 (Paris, 1945): 68–73, 119 ff.
19. James W. Thompson, *Feudal Germany*, 451 ff.
20. S. H. Thomson, *Czechoslovakia in European History* (Princeton, 1943), 7–26.
21. F. v. Šišić, *Geschichte der Kroaten*, I (Zagreb, 1917).

22. The various contributions of Pierre David which showed this in the case of Poland are summarized in his chapter (IV) of the *Cambridge History of Poland from the Origins to Sobieski* (Cambridge, now in print) on " The Church in Poland from its origin up to 1250 ".

23. *See* the distinction between " Südosteuropa " and " Osteuropa " in H. Helmolt's *Weltgeschichte*, vol. 5, and particularly the special *Revue historique du Sud-Est européen*, founded by N. Iorga in 1924.

24. A. A. Vasiliev, *History of the Byzantine Empire*, 1: 111; Ch. Diehl in *Histoire du Moyen Age*, 3: 124.

25. G. Schlumberger, *L'épopée byzantine à la fin du X-e siècle, II Basil II le Tueur des Bulgares* (Paris, 1900); in Toynbee's provocative interpretation that apparent success would be the beginning of the disintegration of the Orthodox Christian society, *see Study*, 2: 369; 3: 26, 147; 4: 392.

26. Toynbee, *Study*, 1: 132 f.

27. In his book on *The Photian Schism—History and Legend* (Cambridge, 1948); his earlier articles on that problem are quoted and discussed by Ch. Diehl in *Histoire du Moyen Age* (Paris, 1936), 9: 443; *see also* the latest summary of his ideas in the article " The Photian Schism in Western and Eastern Tradition ", *Review of Politics*, 10 (1948): 310–331.

28. F. Dvornik, " Western and Eastern Traditions in Central Europe ", *Review of Politics*, 9 (1947): 463–481.

29. This clearly appears in the latest history of that division by P. Jugie, *Le schisme oriental* (Paris, 1943).

30. That expression is frequently used by the Polish historian, J. Długosz (+1480), who otherwise had no special sympathy with Poland's Slavic neighbours.

31. *See* above, Chapter IV, p. 78.

32. That conception was first developed by H. J. Mackinder, *Democratic Ideals and Reality* (New York, 1919).

CHAPTER VII

1. F. Naumann, *Mitteleuropa* (Berlin, 1915), transl. as *Central Europe* by C. M. Meredith (London, 1916).

2. *See* the latest discussion of Haushofer's ideas by Edmund A. Walsh, *Total Power: a Footnote to History* (New York, 1948), 3 ff.

3. *See* the bibliography in Feliks Gross, *Crossroads of Two Continents* (New York, 1945), 141–153.

4. Usually, however, in the equally controversial form: Central and Eastern Europe; for instance, by the " Central and Eastern European Planning Board " whose Secretary General was the author of the book quoted in the preceding footnote.

5. " Mitteleuropa: the Final Stage ", *Journal of Central European Affairs*, 7 (1947): 58–67.

6. *See* the suggestive maps published in the well-known atlas of F. W. Putzger, when under the Nazi régime it appeared in a new, enlarged edition, *Historischer Schulatlas* (Bielefeld–Leipzig, 1942).

7. *See*, for instance, Wilh. Unverzagt's contribution to the book *Deutschland und Polen* (Berlin, 1933).

8. André Chéradame, *Défense de l'Amérique* (Montréal, 1941), 103 f. (" L'Europe centrale, clef du monde ").

9. A particularly striking aspect of that conflict has been recently studied by Z. Wojciechowski, *Polska—Niemcy. Dziesięć wieków zmagania* (Poland—Germany. Ten centuries of struggle. Poznań, 1945), almost completely translated into English in the collective work, edited by the same historian: *Poland's place in Europe* (Poznań, 1947), 85–412.

10. The problem has never been studied as such: there does not even exist any full story of the traditional French-Polish friendship. The Polish Library in Paris started, however, a series of publications on the diplomatic relations between France and Poland, of which one volume appeared before the war: F. de Pułaski et L. Tomkiewicz, *La Mission de Claude de Mesmes, Comte d'Avaux, Ambassadeur Extraordinaire en Pologne* 1634–1638 (Paris, 1937), while a second one was being prepared by the present writer.

11. On the controversial issues regarding the origin of the Swiss Confederation *see* the standard work of W. Oechsli, *Die Entstehung der schweizerischen Eidgenossenschaft* (Bern, 1891) and the analysis of the recent research on that problem by H. Nabholz in the work *Papsttum und Kaisertum* (München, 1926).

12. Best described in H. Pirenne's *Histoire de la Belgique*, 2 (Bruxelles, 1908), Books III and IV.

13. J. Bryce, *The Holy Roman Empire*, 368–370.

14. P. E. Schramm, *Kaiser, Rom und Renovatio* (Leipzig, 1929).

15. The famous statement of John of Salisbury (1160) is most frequently quoted; *see*, for instance, J. W. Thompson, *Feudal Germany*, 383.

16. Gerald G. Walsh, *Dante Alighieri—Citizen of Christendom* (Milwaukee, 1946), 89–91, has rightly observed that Dante is vehement against both Guelfs and Ghibellines; but the latter sin, in his opinion, only by abusing, for party purposes, the right conception of imperial power, while the former oppose that proper conception.

17. First published in 1864; the latest, enlarged and revised edition, cited in the present study, is of 1930.

18. Toynbee, *Study*, 4: 339, 397 where he points out that this artificially restored Empire was neither universal nor permanent, and stresses the superiority of the papal *Respublica Christiana*.

19. R. Holtzmann, " Der Weltherrschaftsgedanke des mittelalterischen Kaisertums und die Souveränität der europäischen Staaten ", *Historische Zeitschrift*, 159 (1939): 251–264.

20. Quoted by S. H. Thomson, *Czechoslovakia in European History*, 44–46, 165–167. A full English translation appeared in the *Slavonic and East European Review*, 26 (1948): 303–308.

21. They had not been included in the Holy Empire after the Partitions nor in the German *Bund* after the Congress of Vienna.

22. This issue, too, is discussed by J. Bryce, *op. cit.*, 432–434 (on the Austrian claim) and 500–502 (on the claim of the Hohenzollern Empire).

23. Adolph Schwarzenberg, *Prince Felix zu Schwarzenberg, Prime Minister of Austria* 1848–1852 (New York, 1946).

24. A. J. P. Taylor, *The Habsburg Monarchy* 1815–1918 (London, 1942), 202.

25. Contrary to the opinion of, for instance, O. Jászi, *The Dissolution of the Habsburg Monarchy* (Chicago, 1929), who, like many others, stresses the internal causes; *see* particularly the conclusions, 453 f.

26. Among the many discussions of the new Austria's vitality *see* Alfred Werner, " Is Austria lebensfähig? ", *Journal of Central European Affairs*, 5 (1945), 109–118, and particularly the final question: " Why should not Austria be able to become as free, democratic, and self-sufficient as the Helvetian Republic? "

27. That was, however, not definitely admitted even by those who defended Austria's independence as a State; *see*, for instance, K. Schuschnigg, *My Austria* (New York, 1938), 12.

28. This is now admitted in all scholarly publications; *see*, for instance, the new *Eastern Review*, published in Vienna in three languages, where the prominent Austrian Slavist, W. F. Schmid, one of the editors, clearly distinguished East-Central Europe, South-East Europe and the Soviet Union, 1 (1948): 7.

29. Feliks Gross, *Crossroads of Two Continents* (New York, 1945), 29–34; *see also* the maps.

30. Bernard Newman, *The New Europe* (New York, 1943), mainly discusses, under this title, the " new " countries between Germany and Russia.

31. Raymond Buell, *Poland—Key to Europe* (New York, 1939).

32. Z. and M. Wojciechowski, *Polska Piastów—Polska Jagiellonów* (Poznań, 1947), try to combine these two interpretations.

33. This is the expression frequently used by Z. Wojciechowski and his school; *see* Maria Kiełczewska, " The Geographical Bases of Poland ", *Poland's Place in Europe*, 12 ff., and the maps illustrating Wojciechowski's own contribution.

34. *See* St. Kutrzeba, " The struggle for the frontiers, 1919–1923 ", *Cambridge History of Poland from Augustus II to Pilsudski* (Cambridge, 1941), 512–534.

35. W. F. Reddaway, *Problems of the Baltic* (Cambridge, 1940), 39.

36. This interpretation still prevails, however, in some of the most frequently used English outlines, to mention only Sir Bernard Pares, *A History of Russia* (last edition: New York, 1944). *See also* the amazing statement by Samuel H. Cross, *Slavic Civilization through the Ages* (Cambridge, Mass., 1948), 51, " that either a White Russian or a Ukrainian is precisely as much a Russian as the purest Great Russian born in the shadow of the Kremlin ".

37. Rudolf Schlesinger, *Federalism in Central and Eastern Europe*, 358 ff., where, however, precisely the Ukrainian and White Russian problems do not receive sufficient attention.

38. N. D. Czubatyj, " Problems of Ukrainian Historiography ", *Bulletin of the Polish Institute*, 2 (1945): 339–352; also his " Ukraine and the Western

World ", *Ukrainian Quarterly*, 3 (1947): 145–158, where he pointed out that this connection with the West lasted until the establishment of Russian rule.

39. G. Vernadsky, *Political and Diplomatic History of Russia* (Boston, 1936); *see* the Preface, p. ii.

40. William H. Chamberlin, *The Ukraine—a Submerged Nation* (New York, 1944), 85.

41. *See*, for instance, N. Iorga, *Histoire des états balkaniques jusqu'à* 1924 (Paris, 1925).

42. J. Kucharzewski, " German Philosophy and the Russian Intelligentsia ", *Bulletin of the Polish Institute*, 2 (1944): 1057–1076; N. Berdyaev, *The Russian Idea* (New York, 1948), 40, 42, 51, 74, etc.

43. *See* Hans Kohn's remarks in his essay on Dostoevsky, in *Prophets and Peoples* (New York, 1946), 133, 139.

44. H. Uebersberger, *Oesterreich und Russland seit dem Ende des XV Jahrhunderts*, I (Wien, 1906).

45. A. Hirschberg, *Koalicja Francji z Jagiellonami z r.* 1500 (The Coalition between France and the Jagellonians in 1500, Lwów, 1882).

46. X. Liske, *Der Wiener Congress von 1515 und Polen* (Göttingen, 1878). There is no more recent study of that important congress in any language.

47. *See* my article " Soviet Russia and the Cordon Sanitaire ", *Thought*, 20 (1947): 87–92.

48. David J. Dallin, *The Big Three* (New Haven, 1945), 111, 119, 123.

CHAPTER VIII

1. L. Varga, *Das Schlagwort vom "finsteren Mittelalter"* (Wien, 1932).

2. Ch. Dawson, *The Making of Europe*, 99.

3. Wallace K. Ferguson, *The Renaissance in Historical Thought—Five Centuries of Interpretation* (Boston, 1948). The growing interest of American scholars in these problems is evidenced in a quarterly newsletter published by Dartmouth College Library for the American Council of Learned Societies: *Renaissance News*, No. 1, Spring 1948.

4. L. M. Smith, *Cluny in the Eleventh and Twelfth Centuries* (London, 1930); André Chagny, *Cluny et son Empire* (Lyon, 1938).

5. Gerald G. Walsh, *Dante Alighieri—Citizen of Christendom; see* particularly Chapter IV.

6. Chapter VII, p. 133.

7. Sometimes even the beginning of the Italian wars, in 1494, is stressed as such a divisive date. Therefore the bibliography in the *Journal of Modern History* covers the period from 1500, considering that the " modern " period started somewhere around this year which itself is less important than the other dates.

8. Etienne Gilson, *Héloïse et Abélard. Etudes sur le moyen âge et l'humanisme* (Paris, 1938); *see* particularly p. 164, where he calls the terms Middle Ages and Renaissance " les symboles abstraits de périodes chronologiques d'ailleurs mal définies ", and Appendix II on mediaeval philosophy and humanism, pp. 225–245.

9. Charles H. Haskins, *The Renaissance of the Twelfth Century* (Cambridge, Mass., 1927); *see*, however, the recent reservations of William A. Nitze, " The So-called Twelfth-century Renaissance ", *Speculum*, 23 (1948): 464–471. A little later a book under the same title appeared in French: G. Paré, A. Brunet, P. Tremblay, *La Renaissance du XII-e siècle* (Paris—Ottawa, 1933), where the term " renaissance " is discussed in the preface by M. D. Chenu, pp. 8–11.

10. That has been pointed out very correctly by Zygmunt Łempicki, *Renesans, Oświecenie, Romantyzm* (Renaissance, Enlightenment, Romanticism, Warszawa, 1923).

11. J. Huizinga, *De herfsttij der middeleeuwen* (Haarlem, 1919—many editions and translations).

12. " Der Staat als Kunstwerk "—this is the title of J. Burckhardt's first chapter in the German original of his famous history of the Renaissance in Italy, first published in 1860.

13. In the first volume of his *Geschichte des Papsttums seit dem Ausgange des Mittelalters*, first published in 1885.

14. H. Rashdall, *The Universities of Europe in the Middle Ages* (1895).

15. Noël Valois, *Le Pape et le Concile—La crise religieuse du XV-e siècle* (2 vols., Paris, 1909).

16. H. A. Gibbons, *The Foundations of the Ottoman Empire* (Oxford, 1916).

17. G. de Lagarde, *La naissance de l'esprit laïque au déclin du moyen âge, II Marsile de Padoue* (Paris, 1948).

18. *The Crusade in the Later Middle Ages* (London, 1938), 463; *see also* his special dissertation on *The Crusade of Nicopolis* (London, 1934).

19. G. Mollat, *Les Papes d'Avignon* (Paris, 1930, 7th ed.).

20. *See* the conclusions of my book *Un Empereur de Byzance à Rome—Vingt ans de travail pour l'Union des Eglises et pour la défense de l'Empire d'Orient 1355–1375* (Varsovie, 1930).

21. Gerald G. Walsh, *The Emperor Charles IV—a Study in Holy Roman Imperialism* (New York, 1924), has characterized his reign from this very point of view; the facts, until 1368, are most complete in E. Werunsky's *Geschichte Kaiser Karls IV und seiner Zeit* (4 vols., Innsbruck, 1880–1892).

22. There is no full history of his long and important reign; *see*, however, the statements of Prince Hubertus zu Löwenstein, *The Germans in History* (New York, 1945), 154 (" once more a true Emperor "), 157. His imperial ambitions have been recently discussed by Ewa Maleczyńska in her (Polish) study on the dynastical policy of the first Jagellonians in *Travaux de la Société des Sciences et des Lettres de Wrocław*, Nr. 5 (Wrocław, 1947), particularly in the chapter " Sub auspiciis Regis Romanorum ", pp. 74–94.

23. *See* James W. Thompson, *A History of Historical Writing* (New York, 1942), 1: 366–370.

24. Pierre Champion (ed.), *Procès de condamnation de Jeanne d'Arc* (2 vols., Paris, 1920–1921).

25. Her biography by Gabriel Hanotaux, *Jeanne d'Arc* (Paris, 1911), is divided into four parts corresponding to the " quatre mystères " in her life.

26. The best history of the battle by O. Laskowski, *Grunwald*, has been re-edited in London, 1941.

27. S. Harrison Thomson, " Pre-Hussite Heresy in Bohemia ", *English Historical Review*, 48 (1933), 23–42; O. Odložilik, *Wyclif and Bohemia* (Prague 1936).

28. *See* my discussion of the information given under that date by the Chronicle of Padua of the Gattari brothers: " Przyczynki genealogiczne do genezy traktatu krewskiego " (Genealogical contributions to the origin of the Krevo treaty), *Miesięcznik heraldyczny* (Heraldic Monthly), 14 (1935): 97–111.

29. Joseph B. Koncevičius, *Russia's Attitude towards Union with Rome* (Washington, 1927), 137 ff.

30. *See* my comparison of the two federations in *Studia historyczne ku czci St. Kutrzeby* (Historical Studies in honour of St. Kutrzeba, Kraków, 1938), 1: 217–232.

31. Recently discussed by Peter Charanis, " The Strife among the Palaeologi and the Ottoman Turks, 1370–1402 ", *Byzantion*, 16 (1942–1943): 292.

32. Its significance in both respects was best understood by the Venetians; *see* Max Silberschmidt, *Das orientalische Problem zur Zeit der Entstehung des Türkischen Reiches nach venezianischen Quellen* (Leipzig, 1923).

33. A. E. Presniakov, *Obrazovanye velikorusskago gosudarstva* (Petrograd, 1918).

34. The unity of that period appears best in the light of the material collected by A. V. Ekzemplarsky, *Velikye i udyelnye kniazia severnoy Rusi v tatarski period*, 1238–1505 (The great and local princes of Northern Russia in the Tartar period, 2 vols., St. Petersburg, 1889).

35. O. Halecki, *Rome et Byzance au temps du Grand Schisme d'Occident* (Lwów, 1937, reprinted from *Collectanea Theologica*, 18).

36. A. A. Vasiliev, *History of the Byzantine Empire*, vol. 2, has an important chapter on that insufficiently studied problem; *see also* R. Guilland in *Histoire Générale—Hist. du Moyen Age*, 9 (Paris, 1945): 400–419.

37. The Confederation of Warsaw was recently discussed by Earl Morse Wilbur, *A History of Unitarianism* (Cambridge, Mass., 1945), 363 f.

38. No defence of Macchiavelli, as recently attempted by Count Carlo Sforza, *Contemporary Italy* (New York, 1944), 8–15, can reduce his tremendous responsibility.

39. Karl Brandi, *The Emperor Charles V—the Growth and Destiny of a Man and of a World Empire* (transl., New York, 1939).

40. Ernest Denis, *La fin de l'indépendance bohème*, 2 vols. (Paris, 1890).

41. *La prépondérance espagnole* is the title of vol. 9 of *Peuples et Civilisations* (new ed., Paris, 1948), by H. Hauser, who covers, however, the whole period from 1559 to 1660.

42. *See* the remarks on Charles Danzay, French envoy in Denmark, by H. Hauser, " Un Français dans la Baltique au XVI-e siècle ", *La Pologne et la Baltique* (Paris, 1931).

43. Two detailed diaries of that Diet are preserved; in English historiography they have been quoted by W. E. D. Allen, *The Ukraine—a History* (Cambridge, 1940), 63, who says, wrongly however, that they were written in Russian: their Polish texts were only published with a Russian translation by the Russian scholar Koyalovich.

44. E. Likowski, *Die ruthenisch—römische Kirchenvereinigung genannt Union von Brest* (Freiburg, 1904).

45. The most detailed discussion of these important events is in the biography of Prince Nicolas Radziwill, then Grand-Chancellor of Lithuania, by J. Jasnowski, *Mikołaj Radziwiłł Czarny* (Warszawa, 1939).

46. In the *Cambridge History of Poland from the Origins to Sobieski* (Cambridge, now in print) these problems are presented both from the point of view of Polish and Swedish historiography by Frank Nowak (Chapter XXI) and V. Törne respectively (Chapter XXII A).

47. They are so typical that Toynbee in his *Study of History* currently uses that term in order to designate similar crises in the history of any civilized society; but it is hardly advisable to change the meaning of that expression as far as Russian history is concerned and to use it for a much earlier period of that history: 1169 to 1478 (*Study*, 1: 53 n. 2; 6: 195 n. 2).

48. Lord Eversley, *The Turkish Empire* (London, 1917). For the exact date and circumstances of Sokolli's death, *see* N. Iorga, *Geschichte des osmanischen Reiches* (Gotha, 1910), 3: 178.

49. That interpretation appears, for instance, in S. Konovalov's *Russo-Polish Relations* (Princeton, 1945), 8: 55–57, and is generally accepted in English historiography; *see* Toynbee, *Study*, 2: 176, and his *Civilization on Trial* (New York, 1948), 168.

50. Recently described in the king's biography by Otto Forst de Battaglia, *Jan Sobieski, König von Polen* (Einsiedeln, 1946), 209 ff., summarized in the author's contribution to the *Cambridge History of Poland from the Origins to Sobieski*, Chapter XXIII.

CHAPTER IX

1. *Journal of Modern History*, 18 (1946): 193–194.

2. William C. Bullitt, *The Great Globe Itself* (New York, 1946), 1 f.

3. This is the title of T. Eckhardt's article in *Thought*, 22 (1947); *see* above, Chapter IV, n. 30.

4. This is the title of a book by Robert M. Rayner, *The Twenty Years' Truce* (London, 1943).

5. Chapter III, p. 61.

6. A penetrating analysis of that controversial problem was given in an appendix to W. Sobieski's *Henryk IV wobec Polski i Szwecji* (*Henry IV with regard to Poland and Sweden*, Kraków, 1910).

7. Franklin L. Baumer, " England, the Turk and the Common Corps of Christendom ", *American Historical Review*, 50 (1944): 27–48.

8. Ross J. S. Hoffman, *The Great Republic* (New York, 1942), 18.

9. Ernest W. Nelson, "The Origin of Modern Balance of Power Politics", *Mediaevalia et Humanistica*, 1 (1943).

10. *See* the remarks of Ed. Perroy in *Peuples et Civilisations*, vol. 7, *La Fin du Moyen Age* (Paris, 1931), 469 f., 474.

11. Chapter VIII, p. 157f.

12. Volume 10 of the collection *Peuples et Civilisations* (L. Halphen and P. Sagnac, ed.) by A. R. de Saint Séyer and P. Sagnac, *La prépondérance française*, 1661–1715 (Paris, 1944), is to be followed by a volume on *La prépondérance anglaise*, 1715–1763.

13. A systematic study of the origin and character of "enlightened absolutism" was started before the last war by the *International Committee of Historical Sciences* and the first contributions appeared in the Committee's *Bulletin*.

14. Arthur H. Buffinton, *The Second Hundred Years' War*, 689–1815 (New York, 1929).

15. *See*, however, the reservations recently made by R. W. Seton-Watson, "The Foundations of British Policy", *Transactions of the Royal Historical Society*, 29 (1947): 61.

16. Lord Eversley, *The Turkish Empire*, 168–190; N. Iorga, *Geschichte des osmanischen Reiches*, 4 (Gotha, 1911), where the Köprili dynasty is discussed in the whole first section.

17. V. O. Kluchevsky, *A History of Russia* (transl. by C. J. Hogarth, London, 1926), 4: 207–229; *see also* Anatole G. Mazour, *An Outline of Modern Russian Historiography* (Berkeley, 1939), 13, 14, 23, 33–34, 59, 60, 93.

18. J. V. Lantzeff, *Siberia in the Seventeenth Century* (Berkeley, 1943).

19. As to the special importance of that city, *see* C. A. Manning, *The Story of the Ukraine*, 51, 71, 106 ff.

20. Sidney B. Fay, *The Rise of Brandenburg-Prussia to* 1786 (New York, 1937).

21. Ferdinand Schevill, *The Great Elector* (Chicago, 1948).

22. R. J. Kerner, *The Urge to the Sea* (Berkeley, 1942), 72–88.

23. The only exceptions were, on the one hand, Poland's interference with Russia's "time of trouble" at the beginning of the century—a unique situation which, as mentioned above (Chapter VIII, n. 49), is usually over-emphasized—and, on the other hand, a last attempt at a peaceful settlement on a basis of equality: the Andrusovo armistice of 1667, confirmed in the "permanent" peace of 1686.

24. From his interference with the election after Sobieski, in 1697; *see* C. Waliszewski, *Pierre le Grand* (Paris, 1905), 88.

25. *See* the chapter "Catharina Constans Invicta" in Robert H. Lord's *The Second Partition of Poland* (Cambridge, Mass., 1915), 153–191.

26. That this constitution was not at all so "crazy" as most historians believe, is well shown in its highly objective study by Paul Skwarczyński in *The Cambridge History of Poland* (Cambridge, 1941), 49–71.

27. "The event which more than any other undermined faith in the balance of power was the partition of Poland", says Alfred Cobban, *National Self-Determination* (Chicago, 1948), 170.

28. *See* my article on " Problems of Polish historiography ", *The Slavonic Review*, 21 (1942–43): 223–239.

29. *See* above, Chapter VII, pp. 130, 138.

30. W. F. Reddaway, " The First Partition ", *The Cambridge History of Poland* (1941), 88.

31. Marian Kukiel, " Kościuszko and the Third Partition ", *ibid.*, 175.

32. This statement by Edmund Burke is quoted, for instance, by Robert H. Lord, *The Second Partition of Poland*, 445.

33. *Ibid.*, 184–190; the discussion in the British Parliament on that problem, in 1791, is also described by Lord Eversley, *The Turkish Empire* (London, 1917), 232–236, and Bronisław Dembiński, *Polska na przełomie* (Poland at the Cross-roads, Lwów, 1913), 430–437.

34. B. Horn, *British Public Opinion and the First Partition of Poland* (London, 1945).

35. *See*, for instance, the chapter " The End of Kozak Liberties " in C. A. Manning, *The Story of the Ukraine*, 131–144.

36. Best shown by André Martel, *La langue polonaise dans les pays ruthènes* (Lille, 1938).

37. As far as the Lithuanians are concerned, this is well described in C. R. Jurgela, *History of the Lithuanian Nation* (New York, 1948), 355–365, in the chapter " The Newcomers ".

38. Hans Kohn, *The Idea of Nationalism* (New York, 1944), Chapter VIII: " Toward the Great Awakening "; *see* particularly 534–560.

39. There even arrived at Vienna, during the Congress, a delegation of the Serb revolutionaries asking in vain for help; *see* Leopold Ranke, *The History of Servia and the Servian Revolution* (transl. by A. Kerr, London, 1853), 207.

40. de Reynold, *L'Europe tragique* (Paris, 1935).

41. G. Ferrero, *The Reconstruction of Europe; Talleyrand and the Congress of Vienna* (New York, 1940).

42. That frequently quoted statement was made in France by Father Gratry.

43. *See* above, Chapter V, p. 99.

44. N. Berdyaev, *The Russian Idea* (New York, 1948), 2, 3, 129.

CHAPTER X

1. *See* the introduction to vol. 1 of *The Cambridge Modern History* (Cambridge, 1902), p. v, and particularly the introduction and the first two essays in his volume, *The History of Freedom* (London, 1922), and G. P. Gooch, *History and Historians in the Nineteenth Century* (London, 1928), 384–385. Lord Acton's *Essays on Freedom and Power* just appeared in a new edition by Gertrude Himmelfarb (Boston, 1948).

2. Bronislaw Malinowski, *Freedom and Civilization* (New York, 1944); *see* particularly the statement on p. 14, and the chapter " Freedom in the Birth and Growth of Culture ", pp. 30–40.

3. *See* M. M. Bober, *Karl Marx's Interpretation of History* (Cambridge, Mass., 1927, a revised edition has just appeared), 80, 86, 180.

4. The mistakes which proved fatal to the Athenian experiment in the field of what we might call international organization, and the discrepancies in their interpretation of freedom have recently been discussed in a provocative article by Sir Alfred Zimmern, " Athens and America ", *The Classical Journal*, 43 (1947).

5. N. Berdyaev, *The Meaning of History* (London, 1936), p. 111.

6. *See* Christopher Dawson's essay on " The City of God " in *A Monument to St. Augustine* (London, 1930), 43–77; also John N. Figgis, *The Political Aspects of St. Augustine's City of God* (London, 1921).

7. *See* his biography by I. Chrzanowski in *Great Men and Women of Poland* (ed. by S. P. Mizwa, New York, 1941), 184–189; he is practically the only Polish historian who receives some attention in the general studies on historiography; *see*, for instance, James W. Thompson, *A History of Historical Writing* (New York, 1942), 2: 637–638.

8. A short outline of his theory, first presented in German (*Die ältesten Beziehungen der Slawen zu Turkotataren und Germanen*, Stuttgart, 1905), was given in the *Cambridge Mediaeval History*, 2 (New York, 1913): 430–434 (" Slavs in German and Altaic slavery ").

9. N. Berdyaev, *The Russian Idea*, 142–144, leads to such a conclusion, although he defends the conception of freedom represented by Orthodoxy (p. 46).

10. Salvador de Madariaga, *The Rise of the Spanish-American Empire* (New York, 1947), tries to show (*see* conclusions, pp. 325–335) that even under Spanish rule there was much less oppression than is usually assumed.

11. Eric Fischer, *The Passing of the European Age* (Cambridge, Mass., 1943), 75 ff.

12. The sociological approach to history appears particularly in the works of Pitirim A. Sorokin whose ideas are briefly summarized in his book, *The Crisis of Our Age* (New York, 1941).

13. Even Toynbee's brilliant interpretations suffer sometimes from such an approach, although he is fully aware of the danger; *see* his essay, " Does History Repeat Itself? ", *Civilization on Trial* (New York, 1948), 29–41.

14. de Reynold, *Formation*, 4: 251, calls that interpretation " le mythe christianisé de la pérennité de Rome ".

15. Typical in that respect is the chronicle of Otto von Freising: *The Two Cities* (transl. by A. C. Evans and Ch. Knapp, *Records of Civilization*, New York, 1928).

16. Particularly under Innocent III; *see* Achille Luchaire, *Innocent III* vol. 5: *Les royautés vassalles du Saint-Siège* (Paris, 1908).

17. C. G. Picavet, *Une democratie historique—La Suisse* (Paris, 1920), 18–27; *see also* G. de Reynold's essays collected in the volume *La Suisse une et diverse* (Paris, 1926). At the very end of the Renaissance period, the United Provinces of the Netherlands, separated from Spain in 1579, offer another, frequently quoted (for instance by E. A. Freeman, *see* above,

footnote 15 to Chapter I) example of federal government, but they did not unite any different ethnic groups with different traditions.

18. *See* my article " Idea jagiellońska ", *Kwartalnik historyczny* (Historical Quarterly), 51 (1917): 486–510, where I opposed the nationalistic interpretation of the Jagellonian tradition.

19. A comparison between these and other mediaeval unions was made by Halvdan Koht, " Vereinigte Königreiche des späteren Mittelalters ", *Wirtschaft und Kultur* (Baden b. Wien, 1938), 503–511.

20. The most recent study in this field is Arthur Nussbaum, *A Concise History of the Law of Nations* (New York, 1947).

21. Quoted by Robert H. Lord, *The Second Partition of Poland*, 199.

22. Otto Hoetzsch, *Russland—eine Einführung auf Grund seiner Geschichte 1904–1912* (Berlin, 1913); in addition to the concluding chapter of N. Iorga, *Geschichte des Osmanischen Reiches* (Gotha, 1913), 5: 614 ff, *see* Youssouff Fehmi, *La révolution ottomane* (Paris, 1911), and the chapter (XXI) on " the Young Turkish Movement " in E. G. Mears (ed.), *Modern Turkey* (New York, 1924), 476–490.

23. Georges Weill, *L'Europe du XIX-e siècle et l'idée de nationalité* (Paris, 1938), is the best survey of that situation.

24. *See* the illuminating discussion of the Bulgarian case by Cyril E. Black, *The Establishment of Constitutional Government in Bulgaria* (Princeton, 1943).

25. That expression by Prime Minister Count Taaffe is frequently quoted; *see* A. J. P. Taylor, *The Habsburg Monarchy, 1815–1918* (London, 1942), 195.

26. J. B. Scott, *The Hague Peace Conferences*, 2 vols. (Baltimore, 1909).

27. *See* above, in Chapter IX, the discussion of Ernest W. Nelson's interpretation.

28. How a Chinese looks on that process was recently explained by Chang Hsin-Hai, " The Moral Basis of World Peace ", *The Annals of the American Academy of Political and Social Science*, 258 (1948): 79–89.

29. *See* the text of this appeal of Aug. 1, 1917, in Harry C. Koenig (ed.), *Principles for Peace—Selections from Papal Documents* (Washington, 1943), 229–232.

30. The origin of article XXI of the Covenant can be best studied with the help of the " Index by articles " in David Hunter Miller, *The Drafting of the Covenant*, 2 vols. (New York, 1928). *See also Taft Papers on League of Nations* (New York, 1920), 318.

31. On the rôle of the Latin American republics *see* Frederick A. Kirkpatrick, *Latin America* (New York, 1939), and Preston E. James, *Latin America* (New York, 1942).

32. Bernard Newman, *The New Europe* (New York, 1943), 17, has rightly emphasized that " more people lived under the rule of their own kin in 1919–1938 than ever did before ".

33. How strongly the prejudice against these " new " nations and their " small " states influenced even the greatest scholars can be seen from a footnote in Toynbee's *Study*, V: 640, where he says that the establishment

of all these *Kleinstaaten* after 1919–1920 created a " no man's land " which the Third Reich seeks to dominate, a solution which in 1939 seemed " perhaps inevitable ". Even more questionable are the " conclusions " of Samuel H. Cross, *Slavic Civilization Through the Ages* (Cambridge, Mass., 1948), 183–185.

34. *Nazi-Soviet Co-operation*, 1939–1941 (Washington, Dept. of State, 1948), particularly Parts III–V.

35. Harry C. Koenig (ed.), *Principles for Peace*, 636–638.

36. Alfred Weber, *Farewell to European History or the Conquest of Nihilism* (transl. by R. F. C. Hull, New Haven, 1948); *see* particularly p. xv. It is significant that the title of the German original is *Abschied von der bisherigen Geschichte* (Bern, 1946), that is " farewell " not only to European, but to all former history.

37. In his essay, " The International Outlook ", *Civilization on Trial* (New York, 1948), 126–149.

38. *See* Toynbee, *Study*, VI: 6.

Index

INDEX

Europeanization of Russia, 88, 92, 97, 99, 171, 174

Far East, 11, 18, 31, 86, 180
Far Eastern Christian civilization, 38, 69
Fay, Sidney B., 45
Federalism, Federation, 14, 86, 89, 108, 120, 122, 127, 131, 134f., 155, 159, 193f.
Ferrero, Guillelmo, 26
Finland, Fins, 13, 93, 98, 113, 121, 135f., 176
Finno-Ugrian peoples, 210
Fischer, Eric, 45, 57, 59
Florence, Union of (1439), 95f.
France, French, 26, 34, 52, 70, 73, 140, 152, 154, 159, 170-3, 180, 206f., 214, 222, 229
Franco-German War (1870-71), 165
Franks, Frankish Kingdom, 28, 112
Frederick the Great, 176
Freedom and Civilization, 185
French Canadians, 58
French historiography, 91, 108
French Revolution, 53, 174, 178f.
Fribourg, 209
Froissart, J., 154

Gallipoli, 76
Gattari, brothers, 226
Gaul, 33f., 40, 111f.
Geneva, 199
Genoa, 80
Georgia, 80
German confederation, 133; *see also* Bund
German Empire, 131, 134, 137, 158, 172, 180; *see also* Holy Roman Empire *and* Reich
German historiography, 90f., 133
Germanic peoples, invasions, 28, 36-9, 90, 121, 130, 133, 176, 187f.
Germanization, 114, 127
Germany, Germans, 7, 17, 19, 27, 34, 36f., 39f., 91, 99-101, 108f., 111-15, 118, 120f., 126, 131, 133-140, 154f., 158f., 173f., 176, 178, 180, 187, 193, 199-201, 206, 208, 212, 223, 230, 232
Ghibellin, 132, 222
Gibraltar, 71; *see also* Straits of
Gilbert, Felix, 126

Gilson, Etienne, 151
Gladstone, William E., 74
Gniezno, Congress of (1000), 39
Golden Horde, 95
Granada, 71
Grand Siècle, 159
Gratry, Father, 229
Great Armada, 158
Great Britain, *see* Britain
Great Elector, 173
" Great Republic ", 51, 169
Great Russians, Great Russian State, 92, 95, 97, 108, 156, 172, 223
" Great Society ", 60, 202
Greco-Roman civilization, world, 10, 14-17, 32, 35f., 39, 45, 47, 55, 60, 72, 80, 188
Greece, Greeks, 13f., 16, 18, 20, 31f., 75-7, 79f., 85, 91, 101, 107, 115-17, 121, 135, 186, 206, 215
Greek orthodoxy, 95, 97, 106, 116f., 138, 155; *see also* Orthodox
Greenland, 69
Grégoire, Henri, 76
Gregory XI, Pope, 153
Grunwald, battle of (1410), 155
Guelf, 132, 222

Habsburgs, Habsburg Monarchy, 96, 120, 133-5, 159, 172f., 178, 196; *see also* Austria
Hague, Peace Conferences, 197
Halich, 94
Hamilton, Alexander, 14
Haskins, Charles H., 38, 151
Haushofer, Karl, 126, 212, 221
Hayes, Carlton, 57
Hazard, Paul, 98
Hegel, Georg W. F., 99
Hellenism, Hellenic civilization, 13f., 32, 46, 48, 58, 91, 186, 188, 206, 208
Hellespont, 76
Helmolt, Hans, 7
Héloïse, 151
Helvetian Republic, 223; *see also* Switzerland
Henri IV of France, 160, 169
Herodotus, 32, 85
Hindu civilization, 208
Hitler, Adolf, 101
Hittite civilization, 208
Hoffman, Ross, 54

236

INDEX

Hohenstaufen, 114
Hohenzollern Empire, 134, 173, 222
Holland, 70, 158, 207; see also Netherlands
Holy Land, 15
Holy League (1684), 169
Holy Roman Empire, 113f., 118–20, 132–4, 152–4, 158, 168, 172–4, 193f., 222; see also German Empire
Holy See, 158, 193; see also Papacy
Holy Synod, 98
Hoetzsch, Otto, 217
Huizinga, J., 70, 151
Humanism, humanists, 14, 51, 53, 60, 147, 194, 224
Hundred Years' War, 154, 159, 171
Hungary, Hungarians, 13, 36, 40, 73, 96, 107, 115, 118, 120, 136, 138, 140, 173, 218
Huss, J., Hussites, 153–5

Iberian countries, peninsula, 40, 57, 70f., 78, 111, 158, 189, 214
Iceland, 68
Illyricum, 111
Imperium Romanum, 14
Incas, 45
India, Indic, 21, 158, 208
Indo-Europeans, 12
Industrial Revolution, 50, 196
Innocent IV, Pope, 94
Iorga, Nicolas, 77
Iranic civilization, 208
Ireland, Irish, 38, 69, 111, 177, 209; see also Eire
Islam, 29, 40, 54, 152, 208
Italy, Italians, 33, 73f., 101, 111–13, 132, 135, 150–2, 154, 169f., 180, 197, 214, 224
Ivan III of Moscow, 96
Ivan the Terrible, 96f., 160

Jagellonian dynasty, Federation, 95, 120, 136, 140, 159, 194, 231; see also Polish-Lithuanian Federation
Japan, 53, 181, 191
Jewish tradition, 206
Joan of Arc, 154
John XXII, Pope, 153
Journal of Modern History, 165, 224
Jullian, Camille, 34
Justinian, Emperor, 72

Kalmar, Union of (1397), 155, 159
Karamzin, N. M., 90
Karpovich, Michael, 89
Kasimov, Khanate of, 218
Kętrzyński, Stanislaw, 210
Kiev, 40, 91, 93, 97f., 172
Kiev, metropolitan of, 94
Kievan dynasty, 93
Kievan Russia, State, 40, 91f., 94, 120
Knights of the Cross, 154
Kolankowski, Ludwik, 218
Köprülü vizirs, 172, 228
Kremlin, 223
Krewo, treaty of (1385), 155
Kucharzewski, Jan, 88
Kulturboden, 129
Kurbsky, Prince A. A., 219

Ladislas, King of Naples, 170
Lapps, 67
Latin America, 56f., 190, 231
Latin civilization, Latins, 14f., 108, 115f., 130f., 138f.
Latvia, Latvians, 118, 136
Lausanne, treaty of (1923), 79
League of Nations, 56, 198
Lebensraum, 129
Lelewel, Joachim, 187
Lenin, W. I., 99
Leo XIII, Pope, 53
Lepanto, battle of (1571), 160
Lhéritier, Michel, 108
Liberia, 73, 214
Libya, 73
limes Romanus, 34, 111
Lippman, Walter, 54
Lithuania, Lithuanians, 94–6, 118, 120, 136, 138, 140, 155f., 211, 229
Little Russia, 94, 108, 136
Livonia, 136, 159
London, 10
Łoś, Stanislaw, 206
Lot, Ferdinand, 26
Lotharii regnum, 112
Louis XIV of France, 159, 171
Low Countries, 131, 134; see also Netherlands
Lublin, Diet of (1569), 159
Lusignans, 74
Luther, Martin, 150
Luxemburg, 131, 134
Lybyer, A. H., 77

INDEX

INDEX

Syria, 41, 74, 208
Szczecin, 101; see also Stettin

Taaffe, Count, 231
Tamerlane, 77, 87, 155f.
Tana, 80
Tanais, 85; see also Don
Tangier, 73
Tannenberg, battle of (1410), 155
Tartars, Tartar Khanates, 93–6, 156, 218f.; see also Mongol invasions
Teutonic nations, 118
Teutonic Order, 154
Thermopylae, 13
Third Rome, 96
Thirty Years' War, 158, 167, 172
" Times of Troubles ", 160, 172, 228
Totalitarianism, 13, 53, 190, 198–200, 202, 206, 218
Toynbee, Arnold J., 3, 9–11, 30, 32, 38, 45f., 52, 54, 58, 60f., 69, 77, 97, 107, 117, 133, 201
Trans-Caucasian region, 87
translatio imperii, 113
Transylvania, 120
Trebizond, 76, 80
Trent, Council of, 157
Trieste, 101
Triple Alliance, Entente, 180
Troy, 75
Tsars, Tsardom, 87, 89, 95f., 98, 100, 108, 136, 178; see also Russian Empire
Tunis, 72
Turanian, 89
Turkey, 79f., 140, 155, 160f., 171f., 176f., 196; see also Ottoman Empire
Turkish historiography, 77
Turks, 74, 76–9, 93, 96, 120, 152, 156, 160, 173; see also Ottomans, Seldshuks
" Twenty Years' Truce ", 167

Uebersberger, Hans, 217
Ukraine, Ukrainians, 92, 94, 98, 100, 108, 136–8, 172, 210, 218, 223; see also Ruś, Ruthenia
Ukrainian historiography, 137, 155, 176, 178, 218
Ultima Thule, 68
Union, religious, 94, 96, 109, 117, 155; see also Brest, Florence

Union of Soviet Republics, see Soviet Union
United Kingdom, 70; see also Britain
United Nations Organization, 56, 60, 201
United Provinces, 131, 230; see also Netherlands
United States, 53, 55, 56, 58, 73, 86, 198–200; see also America
Universal state, 52, 77, 133, 158, 192, 212f.
Universalism, mediaeval, 48, 52, 132, 141, 148f., 152f., 161, 168, 179, 192, 194, 199
Ural mountains, 86f., 99
Ural, river, 86f.
Urban VI, Pope, 153

Valois, Noël, 152
Vasa dynasty, 159
Vasil II of Moscow, 96
Vatican, 96; see also Papacy
Venice, Venetians, 74, 80, 140, 176f., 226
Vernadsky, George, 96, 137, 218
Verona, 214
Vienna, 223
Vienna, battle of (1683), 160, 169
Vienna, congress of (1515), 140, 224
Vienna, congress of (1815), 99, 140, 178–80, 229
Vikings, 38
Visconti family, 170
Vladimir, 92
Volga, river, region, 92–4
Volhynra, 94
Völkerwanderung, 26
Voltaire, F. de, 51, 169
Vorskla, battle of (1399), 156

Wallachia, 120
" War of the Twentieth Century ", 167
Warsaw, 106
Warsaw, Confederation of (1573), 157, 226
Watson, Hugh Seton, 108
Weber, Alfred, 201
West Central Europe, 127, 138, 175
Western Christian civilization, culture, 11f., 14f., 26, 30, 45f., 50, 52, 54, 57f., 60, 80, 97, 107, 115,